HOOSIER PUBLIC ENEMY

HOOSIER PUBLIC ENEMY

A LIFE OF
JOHN DILLINGER

JOHN A. BEINEKE

Indiana Historical Society Press | Indianapolis 2014

© 2014 Indiana Historical Society Press

This book is a publication of the
Indiana Historical Society Press
Eugene and Marilyn Glick Indiana History Center
450 West Ohio Street
Indianapolis, Indiana 45202-3269 USA
www.indianahistory.org
Telephone orders 1-800-447-1830
Fax orders 1-317-234-0562
Online orders @ http://shop.indianahistory.org

Library of Congress Cataloging-in-Publication Data

Beineke, John A.
Hoosier public enemy : a life of John Dillinger / John A. Beineke.
    pages cm
Includes bibliographical references and index.
ISBN 978-0-87195-353-7 (cloth : alk. paper)
1. Dillinger, John, 1903-1934. 2. Criminals—Indiana—Biography. 3. Outlaws—Indiana—
Biography. I. Title.
HV6248.D5B45 2014
364.152'3092—dc23
[B]
                    2013031091

To those individuals, both in the past and the present, who have been victims of violence.

Contents

Acknowledgments

John Dillinger, the Hoosier Public Enemy, was a fascinating diversion to the citizens of Indiana and the nation during the Great Depression. My parents were youths at the height of the outlaw's deeds. In 1934 my father was a twelve-year-old paperboy for the *Indianapolis News*. The newspapers he delivered to homes on the near east side of the city often carried reports of Dillinger's exploits. These included accounts of the bandit's escape from the Crown Point jail, visits to the Maywood home of his sister and his father's farm in Mooresville, and, of course, his numerous bank robberies and getaways.

My mother also had childhood memories of these times. Marion, Indiana, her hometown, had been the site of a bank robbery by Dillinger's future partner, "Handsome" Harry Pierpont. The north-central Indiana city's mayor, Jack Edwards, devoted much attention to protecting his city from the outbreak of lawlessness in the 1930s. Edwards placed roadblocks around Marion, hired additional police, and reinforced the security of the town's banks. When Dillinger struck a bank twenty miles from Marion, Edwards placed the city in a virtual lockdown.

My parents, A. F. (deceased) and Wanda Beineke receive special credit for my initial interest in Dillinger's escapades. The stories they told me as I was growing up in Marion provided the genesis for this book.

Special recognition goes first to Ray E. Boomhower, Indiana Historical Society Press senior editor. He contributed his many talents to shaping and guiding the creation of this work

Boomhower, an exemplary biographer in his own right, generously wrote an illuminating essay titled "A Good Story: Writing Biography" for my book *Teaching History to Adolescents: A Quest for Relevance*. I am also deeply appreciative to Kathy Breen, IHS Press editor, for her confidence in this work in addition to the encouragement and insightful advice she gave in the preparation of the manuscript.

During the research and writing of this book a number of individuals offered inestimable assistance. English instructor at Arkansas State University Brandy Humphrey gave an early draft a thorough review in the area of grammar and syntax and corroborated a number of secondary sources for me. Linda Keller, interlibrary loan librarian at ASU, unflinchingly responded to the many requests I made of her office. Richard Graham, media services librarian and associate professor at the University of Nebraska at Lincoln, verified Dillinger comics sources for me. My son, Colin Beineke, a PhD student at the University of Missouri, listened to my deliberations and provided ideas as I worked on the manuscript. And my wife, Marla, the best unpaid proofreader and gentle recommender of improvements in the editing process, was my most supportive and valuable resource. She is terrific.

Finally, I acknowledge the scholars, historians, biographers, and writers who for the past eighty years have provided their own unique interpretations, insights, and impressions about Dillinger's life. As with the lives of all men and women there is much we know and even more that we do not know. This is true of Dillinger. I have attempted, as I believe is required of all biographers, to use all the available evidence and then tell a factual and compelling story.

When writing about Dillinger, the compelling component was the least difficult aspect of the writing process. The man himself, both living and dead, has always made good copy.

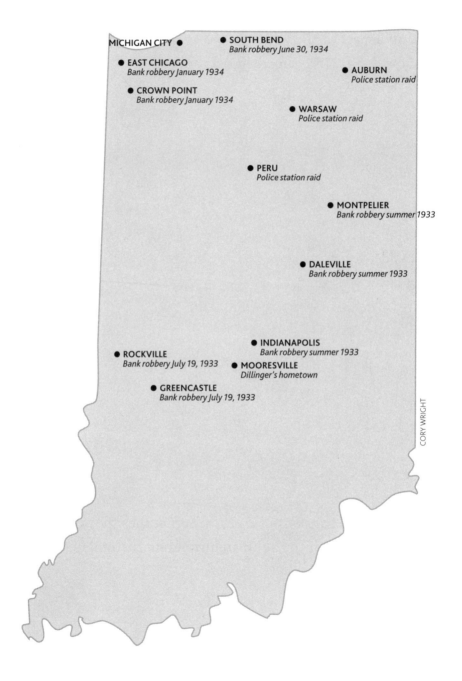

MICHIGAN CITY ●   ● SOUTH BEND
                     Bank robbery June 30, 1934

● EAST CHICAGO
   Bank robbery January 1934   ● AUBURN
                                                    Police station raid

   ● CROWN POINT
     Bank robbery January 1934   ● WARSAW
                                            Police station raid

                              ● PERU
                                Police station raid

                                              ● MONTPELIER
                                                Bank robbery summer 1933

                                       ● DALEVILLE
                                         Bank robbery summer 1933

                              ● INDIANAPOLIS
● ROCKVILLE   *Bank robbery summer 1933*
  Bank robbery July 19, 1933   ● MOORESVILLE
                                   Dillinger's hometown

        ● GREENCASTLE
          Bank robbery July 19, 1933

CORY WRIGHT

Important sites in Indiana regarding John Dillinger.

1

Johnnie

Each bank robbery by John Dillinger was different. Yet all were alike in certain ways. A fast, shiny, new car with four or five men crowded inside would park near a bank. The time was usually near noon or at closing time. A driver stayed with the car, one of the robbers stood watch at the front door, and the other men entered the bank. The bandits were well dressed in suits and hats and had Thompson submachine guns inside their long overcoats. Once inside the robbers ordered the bank customers to line up along a wall or lay down on the floor. Dillinger would then leap over the counter into the tellers' cages. The thirty-year-old robber had a crooked smile, a dimple in his chin, and often made witty remarks as he went about his business. Next, gang members would try to break into the safe. If that failed, they emptied cash from the tellers' drawers into bags or pillowcases. Sometimes they fired the loud submachine guns into the air to intimidate customers.

When either all the loot was taken or the police could be heard arriving, the robbers left. Several customers and employees were used as shields as the bandits made their way back to the car. If there was to be gunfire it usually happened at this point in the robbery. Sometimes gang members, police, and even bystanders were struck by bullets. With hostages both inside and outside the getaway car, the gang would drive slowly out of town. On occasion police and witnesses followed the outlaws, but they never caught them. The Dillinger Gang had struck again.

People still rob banks in the twenty-first century and yet their names are not remembered. No bank robber has been both as celebrated and notorious as John Dillinger from Indiana. Dillinger went about his work during the worst economic times America has ever experienced. These were the hard years of the 1930s, known as the Great Depression. Over a period of fourteen months during 1933 and 1934 Dillinger became the most famous bandit in American history.

Americans enjoyed reading about this Hoosier bank robber. In his book, *The Dillinger Days*, John Toland captured the outlaw's appeal, writing, "No bad man since Jesse James had been so well supported by the public. He robbed banks—not people—and had become to many a sort of Depression Robin Hood. The dash and derring-do of his escapes, his [boldness] to those in authority, and his occasional chivalry during a bank robbery made them see him as folk hero."

Dary Matera, in his book *John Dillinger: The Life and Death of America's First Celebrity Criminal*, noted, "There's never been anyone like John Dillinger before or since. He was indeed America's first, and most enduring, celebrity criminal." For over a year in the middle of the 1930s Dillinger was as well-known as the U.S. president or baseball star Babe Ruth. To some Dillinger was an outlaw, robbing banks and causing violence across the Midwest. To others, Dillinger was a kind of hero, stealing from rich banks and showing that the "little guy" still mattered in an era when poverty stalked the land.

John Dillinger blamed his time in prison as a young man for his turn to crime as a livelihood, telling his father, "I know I have been a big disappointment to you, but I guess I did too much time, for where I went in a carefree boy, I came out bitter toward everything in general."

Hoosier author Kurt Vonnegut gives a short version of the bandit's life in his novel *Jailbird*. Vonnegut, from Indianapolis like Dillinger, was twelve years old when the outlaw reached the height of his fame in 1934. "Crown Point, Indiana is notorious for a jailbreak there by bank robber John Dillinger [who] escaped by threatening his jailor with a pistol made of soap and shoe polish," Vonnegut wrote. "His jailor was a woman. Dillinger was the Robin Hood of my early youth. He is buried near my parents . . . in Indianapolis. Dillinger was summarily executed by agents of the Federal Bureau of Investigation. He was shot down in a public place, although he was not trying to escape or resist arrest." Some of what Vonnegut and others have written about Dillinger is accurate, while other parts can be disputed. Was he a Robin Hood? Was the gun he used at the Crown Point jail a fake? Did he ever kill anyone? Did FBI agents shoot him down in cold blood? Separating fact from fiction is difficult.

During the Great Depression Dillinger and his gangs captured the attention of a nation. At a time when a dime could buy a meal, a ticket to the motion pictures, or a cheap detective novel, the thousands of dollars that Dillinger and his gang stole was considered remarkable. It has been estimated that the half-million dollars taken by Dillinger robberies would be worth seven million dollars today.

If Dillinger's bank robbing was similar to the acts of Robin Hood, then so were the escapes. His breakouts, getaways, and close calls were all part of the story. The escapes he made from jails or "tight spots," when it seemed law officials had him cornered, became the stuff of legends. While the public would never admit that they wanted the "bad guy" to win, many could not help but root for the man who appeared to be an underdog.

Another reason that the name Dillinger still resonates with the public is that his raids on banks coincided with the rise of new crime-fighting methods. These modern approaches were employed by newly created agencies of the government to battle the innovative technologies used to carry out the crimes. While Dillinger was at times compared to the outlaw Jesse James, the tools used in the 1930s were much different than those of the 1880s. Powerful automobiles and modern and deadly weapons were used by the men (and some women) who were labeled as "public enemies."

Dillinger sites in the Midwest.

There was also the Dillinger personality. He was viewed as the gentleman bandit, letting a poor farmer keep the few dollars on the bank counter rather than scooping it up with the rest of the loot. He was polite and handsome. Women liked him. These crooks always seemed to have women, or "molls" as they were called by the press, around them. One of Dillinger's molls, Polly Hamilton, once said, "We had a lot of fun. It's surprising how much fun we had." All this made good copy for newspapers. It seemed like a Hollywood movie and Dillinger was the star.

Although his crime wave took place in the last century, the name Dillinger has never left the public imagination. Biographies, histories, movies, television and radio shows, magazines and newspapers, comic books, and now Internet sites have focused on this Indiana bandit. If the public enjoyed reading about the exploits of these "public enemies" or viewing the newsreels in the movie theaters of that day, so did Dillinger. Ironically, it was outside a theater screening a movie about gangsters that his life ended.

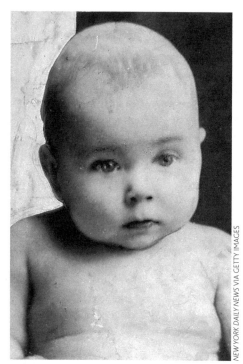

Dillinger as an infant.

Many elements of the Dillinger story are difficult to verify. This is especially true of his early life. After he became famous, many who knew him in his youth, or claimed to have known him, came forth with stories. A number of the episodes in Dillinger's life ring true, while others clearly do not. We know that Dillinger's father, John Wilson, married Mary (Mollie) Ellen Lancaster during the summer of 1887 in Indianapolis. The name Dillinger was at one time pronounced with a hard-G (gur) rather than what we now know as the soft-G (jer). The couple had two children, a daughter, Audrey, born in 1889, and a son, John Herbert Dillinger Jr. on June 22, 1903. Technically the Jr. is incorrect because his father's name was John Wilson. Nevertheless, they were referred to as John Sr. and John Jr. by their family. The elder Dillinger owned a grocery store at 2210 Boyd Avenue and the family home was located at 2053 Cooper Street, now named Caroline Avenue.

Dillinger, at age six (center), on an outing with friends and family.

Audrey married at age sixteen in 1906. In early 1907 Mollie died and Audrey took on the role of mother to three-year-old Johnnie. John Sr. remarried in 1912. His new wife, Lizzie Fields, was from all accounts a good and kind woman. But the young Dillinger's relationship with Lizzie was not always positive. The arrival of a step-brother, Hubert, did not help. As with most children, Dillinger never got over the loss of his mother. "I only wish I had a mother to worry over me, but she died when I was three," Dillinger said later in life. "I guess this is why I was such a bad boy. No mother to look after me."

Dillinger's early years seem to have been quite normal. His sister called their childhood pleasant and her brother was always neat and clean. Some thought Dillinger "cuter" than the other children in the neighborhood. "He wasn't a bad boy," said a classmate. "He didn't do anything other boys wouldn't have done—play hooky or steal cherries." Later, many would look back and construct the story that Dillinger was a "bad apple" from the start.

Teachers found that the young Dillinger had an alert mind and enjoyed reading. But he has also been depicted as a mediocre student. Not caring for arithmetic, he preferred mechanical over academic subjects. The letters he wrote to his family in adult life showed he was above average in reading and writing. Dillinger was quick witted and his father believed he had leadership skills due to his influence over other boys. "Other boys, you know, had stolen change from my desk," said one of his teachers. "But John, although he had ample opportunity to do so, never touched a cent." Another teacher recalled a trait that would become a trademark during Dillinger's career in crime—his politeness. "One thing about him I'll never forget: he always tipped his hat to me," she said.

One story has it that as a kid, Dillinger dressed up on Halloween

A dour Dillinger poses on a fence post on his father's Indiana farm.

*A circa 1915 photograph of a teenage Dillinger and his father on the front porch of the family farm in Mooresville, Indiana.*

like a crook with hat, mask, and toy gun. Cops and Robbers was a favorite game of children in the city and to Johnnie it made no difference if he took the part of the cop or the robber. Games and childhood activities gradually rose from harmless pranks to more serious incidents. Eventually the lure of the streets overcame any interest Dillinger may have had in school. The Pennsylvania Railroad tracks became an enticement too difficult for him to ignore. Dillinger allegedly crashed a switch engine and later began stealing train cargo. Some of the boxcars held liquor that he and his friends sampled. Dillinger reportedly once went to school drunk.

Dillinger's first brush with the law came as a result of the railroad yard temptations. John Sr. was a harsh disciplinarian and did not stop a family friend from taking his son to juvenile court. "If you think it will do any good, go right ahead for I have tried everything," John Sr. told the friend. Just ten years old, Dillinger was brought before an Indianapolis judge for stealing coal from railroad cars. Even at such a young age, he was the picture of a "wise guy," chewing gum, cap resting crooked on his head, and posing in a jaunty stance. His disrespectfulness caused the judge to blurt out in anger, "Your mind is crippled."

Dillinger became a teenager in 1916, the year before the United States entered World War I. His adolescent years were not free from trouble. While never a gang member, he was involved in frequent fistfights. "I knowed kids a whole lot meaner than him," said one of his boyhood friends. "He'd never do anything behind your back— draw a knife or anything like that."

In 1919, when Dillinger was sixteen, he informed his father that he would not enroll that fall at Indianapolis's Arsenal Technical High School. "I'm not going. I'm sick and tired of school and I want a job.

I'm not going and that's that!" he told his father. "Someday Johnnie, you'll be sorry," he replied to his son. "That's my worry," Dillinger snapped back. John Sr. had shifted from the strict, even at times harsh, parent to an easy-going father who let his son have his way.

With school behind him, Dillinger worked at several jobs in a plywood mill. His most consistent job was in a machine shop, where he spent four years. Dillinger was considered a good worker; that is, when he worked. Three or four months at a time seemed to have been his limit. "We liked John very much personally, besides . . . we found him sober, honest and very industrious," said one of his coworkers. "His main trouble [was] he would not stay long." When Dillinger had money, "vacations" from work were frequent. Keeping a job did not seem to be a worry. With business booming during the 1920s, work was never hard to find.

Dillinger moved with his father and stepmother to Mooresville, twenty miles southwest of Indianapolis. John Sr. had purchased a sixty-two acre farm, leaving the grocery business in Indianapolis behind for a new life in rural Indiana. Dillinger, now going by John or John Jr., clearly preferred life in the big city. He commuted to his jobs in Indianapolis by the interurban, an electric streetcar that linked many cities in the state. He later owned a motorcycle and eventually a used Chevrolet.

Even with an automobile, a job, and money in his pocket, Dillinger seemed restless. Living on the farm was not a good match for him. In addition to suffering from hay fever, Dillinger believed that rural life was too slow. The Quaker (Society of Friends) church his parents attended in Mooresville also held no appeal for him. John Sr. noted of his son, "When he wasn't playing baseball he was generally out hunting. He was handy with a gun and a dead shot." Dillinger also enjoyed spending time with his sister's daughter, Mary, visiting the family at their home in Maywood, a neighborhood on the south side of Indianapolis. Mary remembered her Uncle John buying her chewing gum and playing with her during his visits. She found him generous, even tempered, and equipped with a "wonderful smile."

In the early 1920s Dillinger began to read stories of the Old West and watched gangster movies at the local theaters on Saturday afternoons. When he did read it was material about Jesse James, a legendary outlaw often portrayed as a hero who only stole in order to give to the poor, always treating females with great respect. While the major gangster films were not made by Hollywood until the early 1930s, Dillinger did observe stars playing mobsters in the silent pictures of the 1920s. Some think these role models from the Old West and the early twentieth century helped to mold his image when Dillinger began his life of crime.

A view of the Dillinger home near Mooresville.

Older men were another influence at this time in Dillinger's life. While frequenting pool halls in Mooresville and nearby Martinsville and playing amateur baseball, he hung out with these men and was swayed by their wild and sometimes criminal behavior. Martinsville was a place where alcohol, banned under Prohibition, could be secured. But Dillinger was never a big drinker, especially later in his life.

The first major personal disappointment in his young life came when Dillinger fell in love with his uncle's stepdaughter, Frances Thornton. He had always liked girls, even as a child of nine or ten, but this seemed to be true love. First told she could not see John, Frances was later prevented from marrying him by her parents. An angry young Dillinger, possibly in reaction to this setback in his life, borrowed a revolver and on a July night in 1923 stole a late-model car from in front of the Mooresville Quaker Church. Dillinger headed for Indianapolis, only to be apprehended by two city patrolmen. The gun was discovered when he was searched.

In what was the first of many notable escapes in his life, while in the custody of two officers Dillinger slipped out of his coat and fled down the street. The police began shooting at him (an experience that eventually became common) but he escaped. Choosing not to return to Mooresville, Dillinger decided to get out of town by joining the U.S. Navy. Giving a fictitious address, but his own name, he became a sailor. In an official description made of him, the navy found that the young man from Indiana was five foot, five inches tall, weighed 155 pounds, had blue eyes, and brown hair. His vision and hearing were perfect.

Navy life and Dillinger's personality were not a good match. After his basic training in early October, he was assigned duty as a fireman on the battleship USS *Utah*. By late October Dillinger discovered that the hard work of shoveling coal in the bowels of the battleship was not to his liking, nor did he care to take orders. Going AWOL (absent without leave) twice in early November 1923, he was court martialed and punished, all to no effect; Dillinger deserted the navy in early December. The fifty-dollar bounty placed on his head did not bring about his return and the navy soon forgot about him.

With his naval "career" behind him, Dillinger disappeared until the spring of 1924. Back in Indiana, lying to friends and relatives about an honorable discharge from the service, he resumed his old habits of shooting pool, playing baseball, and wasting time. His attention again returned to women, one in particular. Dillinger met sixteen-year-old Beryl Hovious from Martinsville, and within a month the couple was married, tying the knot on April 12, 1924. They lived with Dillinger's parents and later with Beryl's parents.

The marriage was not successful due to Dillinger's habits of staying out late and his inability to find full-time employment. Keeping tabs on the wayward young man became an around-the-clock job for his wife and his father. Dillinger played semiprofessional baseball in Martinsville, but not much else captured his interest. He was indeed restless. When his son was caught stealing chickens, his ever-patient father repaid the farmer. The stakes, though, soon became higher.

Dillinger met and came under the influence of a thirty-one-year-old, ex-convict named Edgar "Eddie" Singleton. The Dillinger family always believed that John went "bad" and his life of crime began due to Singleton's influence. The two men planned to rob a Mooresville grocery store owner, Frank Morgan, of his daily sales receipts. Dillinger, age twenty-one, was to be the "stick-up man," while Singleton drove the getaway car. On the evening of September 6, 1924, Dillinger, carrying a .32 caliber gun and a piece of iron wrapped in cloth, surprised Morgan, who had just closed his store. Hitting Morgan on the head with the makeshift weapon, Dillinger knocked the man off his feet. The elderly grocer came back at his assailant, slapping at the gun, which fired. Surprised by the feisty Morgan, Dillinger, who had probably been drinking, panicked and ran toward what he thought was the getaway car. Apparently also spooked by the events of the evening, Singleton drove off, abandoning his young accomplice.

Demonstrating his inexperience at crime, Dillinger entered a pool hall and began to ask about a gunshot that none of the patrons had heard. The men noticed that the young man had blood on him. Dillinger then returned to his father's farm on foot. By Monday a deputy sheriff had pieced the case together, drove to the Dillinger farm, and picked up the inept robber. Dillinger admitted nothing to the authorities. His father arrived and told his son, "Johnnie, if you did this thing, the only way is to own up to it. They'll go easy on you and you can get a new start. You'll be okay, but you've got to tell them the truth."

Listening to his honest farmer father, Dillinger broke down and confessed to the county prosecutor. Both father and son believed that pleading guilty would bring about leniency on the part of the judge. They were wrong. On September 15, with no attorney, Dillinger admitted his guilt to two counts of assault and robbery. Instead of receiving a light sentence, Judge Joseph Williams gave him the maximum punishment of ten years behind bars. It could indeed have gone easier on the young man. There were a number of reasons for a lighter sentence. These included the fact that he came from a good family, was married, had no criminal record, and that he had been influenced by both liquor and an older accomplice.

It seems, though, the judge wanted to make an example of Dillinger. Although he did assault the businessman, it later appeared that the case against him was weak and the evidence may not have held up if presented in court. For the rest of his life John Sr. second-guessed his decision to have his son plead guilty. He also regretted not hiring an attorney for his son. For years, the issue of the punishment meted out to Dillinger was used as both an excuse and a reason for his life of crime. Even the county sheriff thought the sentence too harsh, saying, "He was just a kid. He got a raw deal. You just can't take ten years away from a kid's life." Dillinger's partner, Singleton, was given a much lighter sentence, enraging both Dillinger and his father.

While the punishment may not have fit the crime, an armed Dillinger had attacked an unarmed, elderly man with the intent to rob him. This episode made it clear that at this point in his life he was not an expert criminal. However, he was quite good at attempting escapes. After the trial Dillinger was transported to the Indiana State Reformatory at Pendleton to begin serving his term. Stopping in Indianapolis for a snack, Dillinger, although handcuffed, turned a picnic table over on the officer guarding him. Taking off on foot with bullets flying over his head, he was captured within minutes.

Dillinger was then taken without further incident to the reform-atory, an over-crowded penal facility that held 2,500 young men no older than their early twenties. Breaking out of his confinement was never far from his mind. Dillinger bluntly told the head of the prison, "I won't cause you any trouble except to escape." True to his word, during his first month behind bars he attempted to escape by hiding in a wood pile. Dillinger was soon discovered and placed back in his cell. There was a predictable attempt to saw his way out through the bars of the cell, but that plan also flopped. After three months "inside" his actions had earned him an additional year to his sentence.

There were, however, periods of good behavior. Dillinger liked to read detective magazines and books on mechanics and sports. There were visits and letters from his family and also his wife. "Gee honey, I would like to see you," he wrote to her. After five years, though, she had had enough. In the spring of 1929 Beryl filed for divorce. No doubt deeply hurt, Dillinger put on a good act in the midst of disappointment. His niece, Mary Hancock, often described him as even tempered, generous to his family, and capable of an engaging smile. Later when he was on the outside, some would

The entrance to the Indiana State Prison at Michigan City, Indiana.
The maximum-security facility had two cell houses with 570 cells and two
dormitories.

The baseball field at the Indiana State Prison.

view the smile as a smirk or crooked grin. Others, though, thought Dillinger had the look of a "killer," and kept out of his way.

Dillinger's hopes were high for a parole in the summer of 1929, but he was turned down. At the age of twenty-six he then made the rather odd request to be transferred to the Indiana State Prison in Michigan City. Located in extreme northern Indiana, this placed him farther from his family. The reason Dillinger gave was that Michigan City had a better baseball team. Michigan City, like any major state penitentiary, was home to hardcore offenders, including bank robbers, safecrackers, gamblers, and killers. Some have suggested this move was all part of John's plan to shift into the big leagues of crime. If so, he would indeed be taught, tutored, and trained by experts. There was no doubt that, with a great deal of time on their hands, the prisoners talked about what they knew best—crime. Dillinger's request for a transfer was approved by the governor and the parole board. For whatever reason, he was on his way to the "Big House."

Although he had chosen to go to Michigan City, Dillinger found the prison far from pleasant. He did the best he could to try to adjust to his new surroundings. He wrote an upbeat letter to his family, even throwing in a religious reference that no doubt met with the approval of his pious father and stepmother: "Now don't think I am an atheist for I am not, I do believe in God, but his ways seem strange to me sometime . . . I will try to pray for Sis, though not that I think it will do her any good. But I would do anything for her. It is nearly church time. I go every Sunday sure am steady huh? J." (He always signed his letters Johnnie, although others spelled it Johnny.)

In his letters Dillinger also referred to sports and mentioned high school and college basketball, a sport near and dear to the hearts and minds of all Hoosiers. "Ben Davis [High School] would sure wallop Mooresville and now [the other prisoners] are giving me the Ha! Ha!—what do you think of Purdue's team this year?" he wrote. Purdue University was where John Wooden, the hardwood star from Martinsville, was playing college basketball and earning All-American honors.

For all Dillinger's talk of sports and church, as 1930 began he could not stay out of trouble inside prison walls. A file was again found on him, he smuggled a watermelon into his cell, and a cigarette lighter and razor were also discovered in his possession. These infractions usually led to trips to solitary confinement. In another letter home Dillinger admitted, "It just seems like I can't keep out of trouble here, of course it was just as bad at the reformatory or nearly so anyway. I guess I am just incorrigible." Indeed he was and his stunts continued. Dillinger foolishly brayed like a donkey and also poured both hot iron and acid on his feet to get transferred out of the manhole cover shop.

Dillinger's time in prison was spent sitting in his cell, taking exercise outside, or working in the shirt factory to which he had been transferred from the foundry. (The supposed baseball playing never panned out for him.) At this time private companies could use prison labor. The Gordon East Coast Shirt Factory was one such business. It appears that Dillinger was actually quite good at attaching collars to work shirts. It was in the prison shirt factory that he met four "professors of crime" who became part of his gang at various times during his criminal career—Harry Pierpont, Charles Makley, Russell Clark, and John Hamilton.

Harry "Pete" Pierpont, due to his good looks, was also known as "Handsome Harry." (Almost everyone at this time had a nickname.) After a bad beginning as a robber, including a woman clubbing him with a T-bone steak during a mugging attempt, Pierpont and his accomplices carried off a number of successful Indiana bank robberies. Finally caught, Handsome Harry was convicted and sent to prison with a ten- to twenty-one-year sentence.

Charles "Fat Charley" Makley was in his midforties, almost twenty years older than both Dillinger and Pierpont. A rather heavy man, Makley had been a bootlegger during Prohibition, and was serving a fifteen-year term for bank robbery. Russell "Boobie" Clark and John "Red" Hamilton both were from Michigan and doing twenty years each for robbery. Hamilton was also known as "Three Fingers" due to the loss of two fingers in a childhood accident.

Another partner in crime that Dillinger met both at Pendleton and Michigan City was Homer Van Meter. A slender but strong man, many viewed Homer as a "clown." Convicted of a variety of

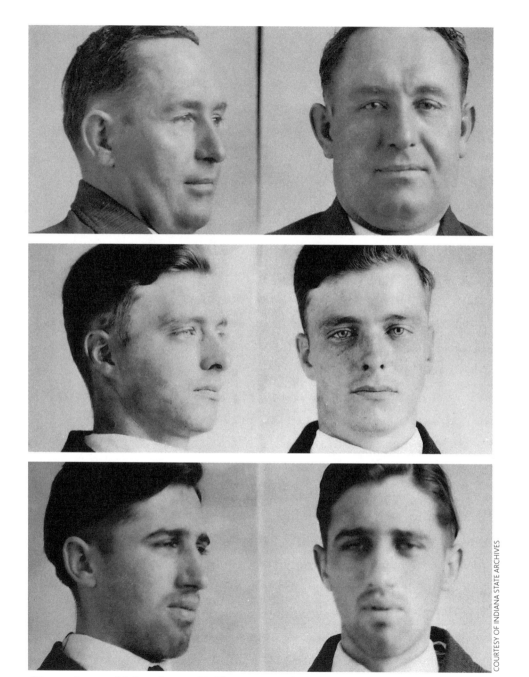

(Top to bottom) Mug shots of Dillinger confidants Charles Makley, Harry Pierpont, and Homer Van Meter.

crimes, it was train robbery that landed him in prison. Behind bars he irritated guards, who in turn knocked out several of his teeth. Van Meter could throw himself out of joint and appear to be crippled. Dillinger found him funny but the authorities clearly thought him dangerous. They would be proven correct. Pierpont found little humor in Van Meter's antics but allowed him to become part of the gang.

Realizing that better behavior was the key to his release from prison, Dillinger became a model inmate. His production of shirts exceeded expectations, which put him in good standing with fellow prisoners Pierpont, Makley, and Clark. He often did their work in return for learning how to rob banks. In April 1933 the Dillinger family filed a petition to the governor for a pardon on behalf of John Jr. Their petition stated that he was needed on the Mooresville farm. (In truth, Dillinger never enjoyed working on the farm and had no intention of helping his father.) It was also noted that his stepmother was in bad health and wanted him home.

The Dillingers had done a thorough job of lining up support for the parole. County officials back in Mooresville, such as the clerk, auditor, treasurer, recorder, assessor, and sheriff, all backed the family's plea. While 188 members of the community also signed on, two key individuals were the former judge, Williams, and the victim, Morgan. Williams made the optimistic but incorrect prediction, "I believe the prisoner has learned his lesson and that he will go straight in the future and make a useful and honorable citizen." After a favorable vote of two to one by the Clemency Board the popular, silver-haired, Democratic governor Paul V. McNutt signed the release order (a parole, not a pardon) on May 9, 1933.

While the release was signed on May 9, Dillinger would not

Joined by his wife, Eleanor, Franklin D. Roosevelt prepares for his March 4, 1933, inauguration as the thirty-second president of the United States.

be free until May 20. Although his help was probably not needed on the farm, his stepmother was indeed gravely ill. John Sr. and Hubert sped to Michigan City in order to get Dillinger home before Lizzie passed away. Upon leaving prison, Dillinger received from the state a cheap suit, five dollars, and a handshake from the warden. Turning for a final look at the prison, Dillinger said, "I'd rather be dead than ever go back in there." Although hurrying from Michigan City to Mooresville, automobile trouble caused the three men to be late; Lizzie died just before they arrived.

The world outside the walls of the Indiana State Prison had changed dramatically while Dillinger was inside. The prosperity of the 1920s had disappeared. Jobs were no longer plentiful. In fact, 25 percent of all workers were unemployed. Men stood in long lines to receive food at "soup kitchens." Farming, manufacturing, business, and the stock market had been in a downward spiral since October 1929. Teachers were not paid, children went hungry, and a few desperate bankers and investors jumped out of tall buildings, killing themselves. The American people decided it was time for new leadership to face what was being called the Great Depression. In November 1932 they voted President Herbert Hoover out of office and elected the Democratic governor of New York, Franklin D. Roosevelt.

Roosevelt's first action upon becoming president in March 1933 was to declare a "bank holiday," closing all banks for four days. Since the beginning of the Great Depression, more than 5,000 banks had failed. That meant there was not enough cash to pay those people who had deposited money in these banks. Banks that did stay open allowed citizens to withdraw only 5 percent from their accounts. In his first radio talk, which became known as "Fireside

Chats," Roosevelt tried to convince the American people that their money was safer in banks than "under their mattresses." That talk came in March 1933. It was now May and former prisoner 14395 of the Indiana State Prison in Michigan City was, like millions of Americans, out of work. But more than 18,000 banks were now open, and Dillinger was ready to begin his new career.

2

Learning the Trade

John Dillinger visited two people when he returned from prison to Mooresville. He called on his ex-wife, Beryl, who had remarried, to supposedly see how she was doing. She asked him to leave. Next he went to see the elderly grocer, Frank Morgan, who he had tried to rob. Dillinger told Morgan he wanted to say thank you for supporting the parole. He also apologized for the attack of almost a decade before, saying that he was going to turn over a new leaf.

The next stop on Dillinger's tour of the community was the local Quaker church, on Father's Day in June 1933. The topic of the sermon was "The Prodigal Son," the old tale of a father accepting his wayward offspring back home. Sitting with his father, the recently released prisoner is said to have quietly wept. The minister said afterward that Dillinger told her, "You will never know how much good that sermon has done me." (Some reported that he had actually slept through the sermon or was working on a list of places to rob.) As for formal religion, Dillinger never attended church again.

With the country three and a half years into the Great Depression, getting a job was difficult. Being an ex-convict made finding employment even harder. But Dillinger did not spend much time looking for work. Within two weeks of arriving in Mooresville he was back in Indianapolis making new friends with an array of shady characters. Elliot Gorn, in his book *Dillinger's Wild Ride*, noted, "He promised everyone in Mooresville that he had learned his lesson in prison. Indeed he had." These "lessons," though, were not the right ones. Within weeks he robbed two grocery stores, a drugstore, and a small bank.

Whether or not Dillinger intended to rejoin society and seek honest work when he was released is impossible to tell. His father's farm was too small to support two men and he had a prison record. There were several reasons Dillinger turned to crime. They included the new knowledge he learned in prison, the fact he had few choices for actual jobs, and finally crime looked like an easier path to follow than real work. He may also have been angry after sitting in prison for nine years.

If it was a new world that greeted Dillinger when he walked out of the Indiana State Prison, it was also a "new" Dillinger, so to speak, that met the 1930s. Dary Matera, author of *John Dillinger: The Life and Death of America's First Celebrity Criminal*, wrote, "Dillinger himself was smarter, trimmer, and more muscular" than before he went to prison, and that "his personality and features [made] him attractive to women and respected by men. Both enjoyed and sought his company." Dillinger started to dress better, wearing fashionable suits and straw boater hats. He also paid for more stylish haircuts. Dillinger became a frequent visitor to the Chicago World's Fair and always took time to attend the movies, his favorite form of entertainment.

Dillinger's release coincided with a national crime wave that lasted approximately two years and changed the face of both crime and law enforcement. While Dillinger became the most infamous, he was not the only crime personality of the time. The Midwest and south central United States was overrun with bandits, kidnappers, and killers. A deadly shootout between federal agents and several criminals at the Kansas City, Missouri, train station in June 1933 started the crime spree. These were the crime figures, both men and women, who became household names over the next two years. They included Charles Arthur "Pretty Boy" Floyd from Oklahoma and George Barnes, known as "Machine Gun" Kelly. The Ma Barker Gang was composed of the wily Alvin "Old Creepy" Karpis and the Barker family. Then there was Lester Gillis, who went by George Nelson. Others called him "Baby Face," a nickname he personally hated. Nelson was the only one of these criminals who worked directly with Dillinger for a period of time.

(Left to right) Infamous American outlaws George Barnes, better known to the public as "Machine Gun" Kelly, and Charles Arthur "Pretty Boy" Floyd.

The national attention that Dillinger drew was still a few months in the future. He gained experience by conducting several robberies after joining an Indianapolis crew of amateur criminals known as the White Cap Gang. (Wearing similar outfits was a typical feature in robberies, as it often caused witnesses to remember the clothes rather than the individuals.) Using borrowed guns and cars, the gang specialized in robbing small businesses, usually all-night grocery stores and drugstores. Planning, if undertaken at all, was done inadequately and the holdups were poorly executed. Few in the gang had experience with guns, and getaway cars were either parked in the wrong places or had inept drivers at the wheels.

One night the White Cap Gang was actually chased by police before the robbery even began. They eluded the law that evening but damaged the getaway car in the process. Another robbery went out of control, and so did Dillinger. An elderly grocery owner froze when the bandits entered, and he failed to follow directions. In a flash of anger, Dillinger smashed the end of his gun into the old man's face, breaking his dentures and splattering blood and teeth onto the floor. There were one or two other such incidents reported early in his criminal career. On one occasion Dillinger took a swing at a man and during another robbery shot his gun into the air. Such episodes were not the usual behavior for the future "gentleman bandit," as Dillinger was later portrayed in the press.

The money stolen by the White Cap Gang robberies was not large—some takes were as little as thirty dollars. Dillinger soon tired of the petty activities of these small-time operators. He had bigger plans in mind. Needing transportation, Dillinger found a 1928 Chevrolet coupe with red-wire wheels and purchased it for $250. Always rather bold (and maybe a bit foolish), he asked the car dealer if an ex-convict could get a driver's license. Dillinger, wanting to move up in the world of crime, then quit the White Cap Gang. He realized they were too amateurish and their ineptness would, he believed, eventually land him back in jail. Dillinger also felt a loyalty to his former prison mates in Michigan City. Loyalty would be a familiar trait during his career in crime. Money from robberies was channeled to lawyers or used to bribe officials in helping his friends still in prison in northern Indiana. These men would return the favor when the tables were turned and Dillinger was again jailed. The saying "honor among thieves" seemed to have held true in the case of Dillinger and his associates.

Dillinger had a list of possible banks and businesses given to him by fellow prisoners when he left Michigan City. Unfortunately for Dillinger, many of the banks and businesses had closed, victims of the Great Depression. After an embarrassing episode or two with defunct or nonexistent banks, he decided to do his own organizing. All the while Dillinger, who turned thirty years old on June 22, 1933, had regular meetings with his parole officer. With a straight face he told the man he was looking for work and helping his father on the farm. Neither story, of course, was true.

Dillinger realized high-stakes robberies would call for increased firepower. While he always carried a handgun, he became fascinated with the newer, high-powered weapons. He was also becoming more skillful at driving. One time in his recently acquired Chevrolet, he and a partner were spotted by the police. In an instant Dillinger stopped, put the car in reverse gear, and drove the car in the opposite direction. The passenger later remembered that Dillinger could drive an automobile "faster [backward] than some people drive forwards."

In early June 1933 Dillinger and two of his Indiana buddies robbed the New Carlisle National Bank in northern Ohio. The three men, all wearing handkerchiefs as masks, had been hiding inside the bank when a bookkeeper arrived. "All right, buddy, open the safe," said Dillinger. As they went about filling their bags with money, a female clerk walked through the door. In what would become a trademark of his robberies, Dillinger was courteous to a fault. He placed a cloth on the floor for the woman before having her lay down. Having bank customers and employees lie on the floors or stand against the walls was a common practice. This would keep pedestrians outside from observing what was going on inside the bank. When two more employees walked in Dillinger greeted them by saying, "You hadn't ought to come in the bank so early." He frequently employed such quick wisecracks.

The gang's $10,000 take was not enough for the newly freed Dillinger. Returning to Indianapolis the same day, the men robbed a drugstore and a grocery. Dillinger and a partner argued over where the employees and customers should look while being robbed, giving the employees different directions. As they left the grocery their getaway driver had parked the car in a poorly chosen spot and then forgot to pick up the third member of the party. They returned, picked up the stranded gang member, and drove off, arguing with each other. They gained little money from either business showing the group's inexperience. It was not an impressive start to a career in crime.

Indiana was an active state for bank robbing, ranking fourth in the nation. Hoosier bankers had to pay ten times as much for holdup insurance as banks in other states. In 1922 and 1923 there were forty-eight robberies in Indiana alone. Twenty bandits rode into

Spencer, Indiana, cut phone wires, tied up the sheriff, and blew open two safes. One robber hit the same bank so often it was reported that he would walk in and say, "You know who I am and you know why I'm here." The Indiana Bankers Association, frustrated with the lack of help they were getting from the law, suggested members arm tellers and give them weekly target practice.

In late June Dillinger and a partner tried to rob a factory on pay day. It was a flop, and an employee at the factory was wounded when one of the robbers dropped his gun and it accidentally fired. Dillinger also spent some time in Kentucky and may have robbed more than one bank in that state. As would often be the case, though, he was given credit for jobs he never pulled off.

Dillinger's next bank robbery was July17, 1933, in Daleville,

INDIANA HISTORICAL SOCIETY, BASS PHOTO COLLECTION, P 130

Bank tellers and staff at the National City Bank in Indianapolis, circa 1922. Banks such as this one in Indiana were often easy pickings for Dillinger and other criminals.

Indiana. He had kept in touch with one member of the old White Cap Gang, Harry Copeland. The two men had hit a tavern in Muncie, Indiana, two days before but gained only seventy dollars. Finally realizing there was more money in banks, Dillinger decided to focus his full-time attention on them. It was with Copeland as his partner on a hot, summer afternoon that Dillinger walked into the Daleville bank, showed a pistol, and courteously and calmly said to the female teller, "Well honey, this a holdup. Get me the money." Not satisfied with the coins and small bills being handed over, he asked for access to the teller's cage. When told there was no key, Dillinger launched himself over the counter. This would become another of his well-known trademarks—the quick and graceful vaults over counters that were often several feet high. The feat earned him the nickname "Jackrabbit" in some newspapers.

The total from the Daleville bank was only $3,500, but Dillinger and Copeland made an easy getaway. Before leaving, the pair asked the employees and customers to step into the vault and they closed the door. In addition to coins and currency they stole a cache of jewelry. Dillinger's confidence was growing. After they left, a female teller opened the vault from the inside. For this young woman it was the experience of a lifetime. She later said, "I think he knew I was a kid and was sorry to scare me. He didn't want to scare me any worse than he had to." She found Dillinger to be quite "courteous." Although the bank later relocated, for many years a misspelled sign on the building read "DILLENGER WAS HERE."

Dillinger was proving skillful at robbing banks. Astounded by their own success, two days later, on July 19, Dillinger and Copeland robbed the Rockville National Bank in western Indiana. This time things did not go smoothly. The bank president's son,

hearing the robbery taking place from another room, retrieved a
.38 Colt revolver. Opening the door slightly, he took one shot at
Copeland, barely missing him. Dillinger entered the room, placed
his gun in the shooter's stomach, and pulled the trigger. Although
it clicked, Dillinger's gun did not go off. He left the young man and
went back to finish the job. By the time they had swept the teller's
cage clean, their yield was a measly $140.

Always a lady's man, Dillinger next decided to take a break and
visit the sister of a Michigan City inmate he had met in prison.
Separated from her husband, and the mother of two children, Mary
Longnacker lived in Dayton, Ohio. Dillinger's letters to Mary used
what might be called "movie talk." He wrote, "Honey, I miss you
like nobody's business and I don't mean maybe." Dillinger went
on, "I fell for you in a big way . . . and that isn't a lot of hooey." The
language could have been taken from a Hollywood gangster film.

Dillinger decided to take Mary and a friend of hers to the
Chicago World's Fair in late July. He had been there earlier in the
month and visited the event whenever he had the chance. A grand
time seemed to have been had by all. Photographs were taken and a
policeman even posed with Mary as Dillinger took a picture of the
group. Before returning to Dayton, Dillinger splurged and bought
her a new dress.

The clearly smitten bank robber daydreamed of moving to South
America with Mary and her two children. Trying to push Mary's
divorce proceedings along, Dillinger unwisely visited her husband's
place of work. The two men quickly got into a fistfight. The town
constable was called and took Dillinger into custody. The unarmed
officer, clearly not knowing who he was dealing with, placed his
arrestee behind the wheel of his own car, jumped on the running

board, and told him to drive into town. Dillinger floored the accelerator and then slammed on the brakes, knocking the lawman onto the street and then sped away, escaping with ease.

With the situation too hot to remain in Dayton, Dillinger decided to visit his sister, Audrey Hancock, in Indianapolis and his father in Mooresville. Whether Dillinger's parole officer had connected him with the series of robberies is unclear, but he had decided to pick his parolee up for possible violations. In what became known as "Dillinger's Luck," two deputies, ordered to watch Audrey's home, had fallen asleep when he made his visit. Dillinger eluded his parole officer again at the farm in Mooresville, this time leaving a birthday present of a shirt and tie for his father right under the official's nose.

Putting romantic and family affairs on hold, Dillinger decided to return to "work." His next target was in the small eastern Indiana town of Montpelier. On August 5 Dillinger, Copeland, and an unknown driver pulled in front and entered the National Bank of Montpelier. Seemingly more comfortable and at ease in his new vocation, Dillinger casually walked into the bank. Chewing gum and with his gun in clear view, he smiled and said, "This is a stick up." Again he jumped over the cashiers' railing and shoveled more than $12,000 into a sugar sack. A newspaper story about the robbery said the trio left only forty cents behind. Dillinger wore no mask, only his straw boater hat and a well-tailored suit. Roadblocks, a ploy that never seemed to work when Dillinger was involved, were placed on roads to the two largest nearby towns, Marion and Hartford City. The robbers escaped, though, by some other route.

The Montpelier raid was a risky move by Dillinger. A holdup attempt at the same bank by another gang two years before had resulted in the death of one bandit and the capture of the rest of the gang. In addition, the police and mayor had offices in the same building as the bank. Dillinger rented a string of apartments in East Chicago, Indiana, and began casing other banks. This was all proving to be, the newly minted criminal thought, a bit too easy. But that feeling did not last. If not yet known on the national scene, Dillinger was beginning to capture the attention of state officials.

The first lawman who realized Dillinger was a serious threat to public safety and bank deposits was Matthew "Matt" Leach, captain of the Indiana State Police and second in command to the agency's superintendent. An immigrant from Serbia, the thirty-nine-year-old Leach was a World War I veteran who had, before the war, ridden with General John J. "Blackjack" Pershing in pursuit of the Mexican revolutionary bandit Pancho Villa. The ISP was neither a

Indiana State Police captain Matthew "Matt" Leach.

large nor modern organization. Leach had less than ninety men to cover the state's ninety-two counties.

Leach entered into the chase for Dillinger early in July 1933. The stunt of leaping over bank railings actually gave Leach the first inkling the banks were being robbed by the same bandit. His inability to catch his man made the ISP leader a source of ridicule. John Toland called the ongoing pursuit of Dillinger by Leach "one of the most remarkable personal duels ever waged between lawman and criminal." "Two Minutes Late" Leach, as some called him, was said to have always reached the scene just in time to glimpse Dillinger's coattails. One time when visiting the Dillinger farm to question John Sr., the son had just left. So the chase would go for Leach over the next year.

Dillinger, especially, thought his pursuer inept. After attending a gangster film where a detective was depicted as dim-witted, he told his buddies, "You should have been with me, Matt Leach was in the picture." Leach would be the butt of jokes for the next year as he pursued Dillinger. Leach was a stutterer, a disability Dillinger callously ridiculed whenever he had the chance. The outlaw called Leach, imitated his stammer, and then hung up. A coworker reported that when the angry and frustrated Leach was not stuttering he was cussing. Leach was often unlucky and misinformed as he pursued Dillinger. Information he provided to the press only seemed to make Dillinger and his gangs look smarter than the police. Leach told the story of Dillinger associate Homer Van Meter being stopped by the police. Van Meter actually talked the officer into demonstrating how their two-way radio worked and then drove away. Van Meter was an accomplished speaker. He basically "talked" his way out of prison with an impressive letter to the parole board explaining how he had reformed while behind bars.

Leach's failures were not always his fault. He was, after all, on the right side of the law. He employed modern approaches to fighting crime such as the science and psychology of criminal behavior. The ISP had also become more organized. For example, it began to keep files on criminals, traced all mail going to Dillinger's relatives in Maywood and Mooresville, and later placed wiretaps on the

telephones. Handwriting samples for Dillinger had been secured and
comparisons were made on all first-class mail sent to Mooresville
in hopes of tracking him down. Surveillance of places Dillinger had
frequented before his crime spree were also put under watch. In
spite of all these efforts, Leach still came up empty-handed.

While the police were working their end of the case, Dillinger
was busy building a network to preserve his freedom. To this day
the full story of his possible connection to the law enforcement
establishment is not fully known. He may have been able to bribe
unscrupulous officials, especially local police detectives. Most
likely Dillinger received tips concerning traps being set for him. A
connection to East Chicago police has often been suggested, but solid
evidence to support the allegation has never been verified. No doubt

*Indiana governor Paul V. McNutt gets his fingerprints taken by a member of
the Indiana State Police at the 1935 Indiana State Fair.*

emboldened by his successes, Dillinger increased the number of his gang and also began to employ the methodical approach to bank robbing he had learned in prison. This, along with newly available technologies, made him a formidable adversary for lawmen.

Bank robberies had begun in the nineteenth century, but did not become an issue for law enforcement until after World War I. At about this time, a German immigrant named Herman Lamm introduced a new, systematic approach to robbing banks. The Lamm Method had a number of stages. These included "casing" or studying how the bank operated. Various men were used for assorted duties—the lookout, the inside men, and the getaway driver. Robberies were also timed and rehearsed. Planning was

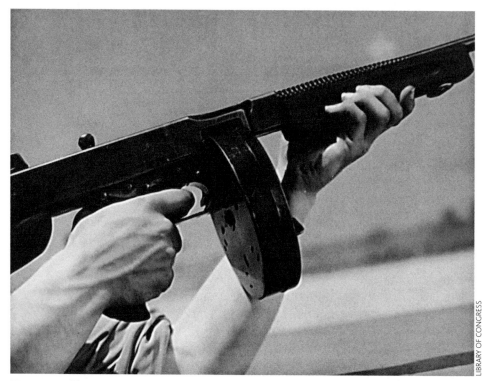

The .45-caliber Thompson submachine gun being test fired at Fort Knox, Kentucky.

the key. The getaway was a critical element of the Lamm Method and became an art unto itself. Bandits usually used stolen cars for the actual robberies. They later exchanged the stolen vehicle for another car several miles from the scene of the crime. Sometimes it was their own automobile, sometimes not. As they drove from the scene of the crime, they threw roofing nails from the back of their car to hamper those in pursuit. With cars of the day equipped with tube tires and thin treads the tactic often worked. Finally, the escape route was carefully planned in advance, usually avoiding major highways. Dillinger thoughtfully studied all of these methods while in prison.

Several new technologies played a major role in bank robberies. The part that technology contributed in the success of Dillinger's life of crime cannot be overemphasized. Technology, when it finally found its way into the hands of law enforcement, eventually turned the tide against criminals. At the time that Dillinger and other felons were making their mark on America though, the technology was in their hands, not in the hands of those on their trail.

The weapons available at this time are the most obvious examples of these technologies. While handguns were becoming more sophisticated, it was the automatic rifle that had advanced most in the field of firearms. The Thompson submachine gun was named for General John T. Thompson, who invented it during World War I. The original purpose of the submachine gun was to be a miniature machine gun small enough for a man to carry "over the top" of the trenches toward the enemy. If they arrived at the enemy line, soldiers used the Thompson as a "broom for sweeping the trenches." But the weapon was used very little during the war.

The deadly gun was also known as the "Tommy Gun," "Chicago

Typewriter," and the "Chopper." It was actually a machine pistol attached to a rifle barrel that could fire at a rate of 800 bullets per minute. But no metallic cylinder (magazine) or drum attached to the gun could hold that many bullets. They were considered automatic because they fired repeatedly when the trigger was held, allowing for a burst or spray of bullets. The Thompson was considered deadly because it used large .45-caliber bullets that came from fifty- or 100-round drums. There was also the noise. These weapons were extremely loud whether fired inside a building or out in the open. To citizens inside a bank or walking down the street, the sound of these guns could be enormously intimidating.

As the 1920s came to a close, the Thompson submachine gun was well-known among the public as the gangster's weapon of

John M. Browning (left) studies his invention, the Browning Automatic Rifle, with a Mr. Burton of the Winchester Repeating Arms Plant in Connecticut, circa 1918.

choice. William Helmer, author of *The Gun That Made the Twenties Roar*, wrote "Along with jazz, flappers, bathtub gin, speakeasies, one-way rides, and bulletproof limousines, the Tommy Gun became a familiar symbol of America's 'Roaring Twenties.'" The submachine gun became a trademark of important outlaws, its firepower giving them a tremendous advantage. Helmer believed that the military and police ignored the Thompson until gangsters and bank robbers started using it. Near the end of his life Thompson, the gun's inventor, wrote with regret, "It has worried me that the gun has been stolen by evil men, and used for purposes outside our motto, 'On the side of law and order.'"

An additional weapon used by bandits and gangsters in this era was the Browning Automatic Rifle, or BAR, designed by John M. Browning in 1917 and used by the Clyde Barrow gang of Bonnie and Clyde fame. With either .30- or .50-caliber bullets, the BAR rivaled the Thompson in the damage it could wreak. Both the BAR and the Thompson were fairly easy to conceal in a long overcoat or alongside the leg. They were also carried in musical instrument cases or pillowcases. The weapons weighed a relatively light eight to ten pounds.

Another technology that put the police at a disadvantage was the type of automobiles the crooks used. At this time, as with weapons, lawmen seemed to have less powerful cars than those they were pursuing. Possibly due to cost, almost all police and sheriff departments used four- or six-cylinder Fords, Chevrolets, or Plymouths. Bank robbers usually purchased or stole V-8 Fords and Hudson Essex-Terraplanes, a box-shaped auto with a small trunk, large seventeen-inch wheels, and an eight-cylinder engine. Dillinger almost always drove the Terraplanes, while Bonnie and

Dillinger's 1933 Essex-Terraplane, on display at the Indianapolis International Airport in 2013.

Clyde preferred Ford V-8s. The larger engines allowed the Fords and Terraplanes to travel at speeds of almost ninety miles per hour. There were a few cases where getaway cars were "souped" up and could reach 100 miles per hour. These cars were fast considering the winning speeds for the 1933 and 1934 Indianapolis 500 was 104 miles per hour. Some of the men who took the wheel of these high-powered machines during getaways were former racecar drivers. But the ability to deftly handle these powerful machines was a skill that Dillinger and most of his cohorts possessed themselves.

Bulletproof vests were also used by bank robbers. These heavy over-the-shoulder garments had numerous pockets into which lead bars were placed. Some of them were lined on both the front and the back. Able to withstand all but the most high-powered bullets, these vests saved the lives of Dillinger and his gang on more than one occasion.

Some emerging technologies worked against the crooks. One of these was communication. Commercial radio came into its own in the 1920s as a means of home entertainment and news. Some law enforcement agencies had one-way radios capable of transmitting in a single direction. These signals were called "all points" bulletins. This was not much help, though, if one did not know where the "points" were being sent from or who was on the receiving end of the messages. And few if any receivers were in police cruisers. Bank robbers did not have radios either, but they did undertake careful getaway plans using side roads or heading in the opposite direction the police may have guessed. There were a few two-way radios, but they were not commonly used by the police until the 1940s.

Banks worked to thwart robberies, using "marked bills" to track stolen money. Marked bills were actually currency that the bank had a list of by serial numbers. Bank alarms were also introduced. These alarms were attached to buzzers under counters that cashiers would press alerting police stations a robbery was under way. Safes and vaults were placed on timers that only opened at certain times of the day. Also, bulletproof glass compartments holding armed guards were installed in some bank lobbies.

Near the end of Dillinger's crime spree, airplanes came into limited use. If the authorities knew which direction the crooks were heading, if an airplane and pilot could be secured, and if the weather was clear, then tracking the getaway car from the air could prove effective. In addition, new crime-fighting techniques were being used by federal agents to track down and identify criminals. Accountants were used to look into bank and tax records, fingerprinting became a major tool for lawmen, and firearm experts added their talents to the pursuit of criminals. These approaches were equally helpful in locating the stolen money and using the evidence gathered to convict suspects in courts.

Dillinger and robbers like him were nevertheless successful. Republican controlled state governments in the 1920s had been stingy when it came to spending funds. Money to support law enforcement had been severely reduced and as crime rose police were not ready to deal with this new breed of criminals. Some bankers, therefore, had to hire their own detectives, while police often allowed untrained volunteers to become deputies.

As July 1933 turned into August, Dillinger shifted from Indiana to hitting banks in Ohio. With a new gang of five, not the one or two men that had been his accomplices before, the Hoosier bandit arrived in Bluffton, Ohio, on August 14. He now had a fast car and heavy armaments. In a way, bank robbery could be described as controlled chaos. For example, it was often difficult to know the actual number in a gang. After a robbery witnesses differed about whether a particular robbery was undertaken by four, five, or even six men. Each of the men in the gang had a role to play in a bank job. Two or three of them would go inside the bank with another man stationed at the door. The two other men would be on the street with one, usually the driver, close to the getaway car. Five was not necessarily a perfect number. Three was usually a minimum and sometimes the additional personnel only added to the confusion when events got out of control, which happened on occasion.

The Citizens National Bank of Bluffton was one place where new technology was in use to respond to the robberies shocking the Midwest. (It should be noted that credit for the mid-August

1933 robbery by Dillinger is disputed.) This particular Ohio bank had installed a timer on its safe, which changed the outcome of the robbery. The man accompanying Dillinger inside the Bluffton bank asked for change for a five-dollar bill. He then stated, "This is a stickup." At this point Dillinger sprang over the six-foot-high bank

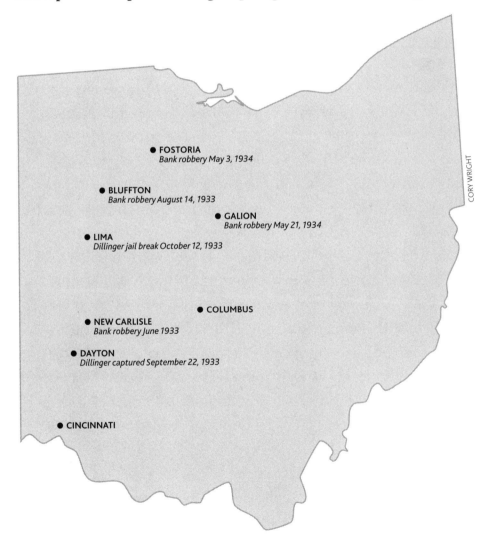

Dillinger sites in Ohio.

cage and ordered the tellers to fill a pillowcase with cash. Unhappy with what was being placed in the makeshift sack, Dillinger said, "You've got more money in here. Where is it?" The rest of the money was, he discovered, inside the locked, timed vault. This limited the take and no doubt frustrated the gang.

A second bank technology then came into play—alarms. These alarms were either connected by wire to police stations or to bells attached to the outside walls of the building. Someone in the Bluffton bank had pressed the buzzer, causing the alarm to begin clanging outside. A city waterworks whistle then went off, adding to the commotion. Becoming extremely nervous Dillinger's inside partner said, "They're after us. Let's go!" Another trademark of a Dillinger bank job was the calm and relaxed manner of the gang's leader. "Take it easy. We've got plenty of time," he coolly responded.

To add to the confusion, gunfire erupted outside. One of the gang on the street had fired his machine gun into the air to push back the crowd gathering around the bank. Foiled by the vault timer, Dillinger left the premises with a paltry $2,100 and a handgun. The five men loaded into their getaway car, shooting their automatic weapons over the heads of the crowd as they drove away. The police never arrived at the scene and the event was so unsettling that witnesses could not even identify the make of the automobile carrying the crooks. From beginning to end the robbery lasted five minutes.

The phrase "one step ahead of the law" held true for most of Dillinger's career. As noted, John Sr.'s mail was being tracked and his sister's home watched. Meanwhile Leach was in Kentucky following dead-end leads. Other law enforcement officials were searching possible gang hideouts in northwest Indiana. While not able to guess Dillinger's next target, officials discovered that he usually drove a Hudson Essex Terraplane. The automobiles used in robberies, however, were often stolen and discarded after the crime.

The investigations and resulting publicity of the robberies created a circus-like atmosphere at times. What became a never-ending series of "Dillinger sightings" began when he was blamed for a Grand Haven, Michigan, bank job on August 18. The heist was in fact carried out by Gillis, now well-known as George "Baby Face" Nelson. Nelson hooked up with Dillinger and his gang the following year. Nelson had been what society was beginning to refer to as a juvenile delinquent. A reform school alumnus, as well as a former guest of the Joliet State Prison in Illinois, most of Nelson's brief life had been one of crime. There was one difference between Nelson and other criminals of this time—he was happily married and the father of a son and daughter. He also did not drink, smoke, or gamble. Personal traits aside, Nelson, as will be seen, was clearly mentally unbalanced. Nelson, it was said, killed just for the thrill of it.

In late August Leach heard that Dillinger was in Gary, Indiana. This tip was actually true. But by the time Leach arrived in northern Indiana, Dillinger was gone. For the crook it was almost like a game, for the lawman it was serious business. In what had become a series of phone calls, Dillinger rang Leach and said, "You almost surprised me in Gary, gumshoe [a term of ridicule toward policemen]. Nice try." Dillinger returned to Indianapolis, where Leach was headquartered, on September 6, with a smaller gang of only three men. The hometown boy robbed the Massachusetts Avenue State Bank of $24,000. There was no mistaking who the perpetrator was this time, as Dillinger vaulted over the bank cages in acrobatic fashion and took his time removing all the cash. The gang then departed for Chicago, the city to which Dillinger returned often over the next year.

Jeffrey King has written in his book, *The Rise and Fall of the Dillinger Gang*, that the gang's leader had "caught the public's fancy because, even in the face of death, he exhibited poise, bravery, self-confidence, and a sense of humor." The public also, according to King, felt sorry for him due to the seemingly unfair prison term. "In the minds of many struggling Americans, the same thing could very well have happened to them," wrote King.

Helmer has given a concise description of why Dillinger was beginning to be seen as a hero in the eyes of some: "Inside a bank he remained composed and business-like despite flying bullets, hysterical customers, clanging alarms; in escaping, he treated hostages with good-humored courtesy and released them unharmed." Less than three months after leaving prison, Dillinger had successfully applied the skills and knowledge he had learned inside the walls of Michigan City. In addition, he added to those tools physical ability, self-confidence, good looks, and a dashing personality that made him a natural for the role of a modern bank robber in 1930s America.

3

Caught—But Not for Long

In September 1933 John Dillinger paused in his string of successful robberies to take care of two other pieces of business, one professional and one personal. Although free for the past four months, Dillinger had not forgotten his former cellmates inside the Indiana State Prison at Michigan City, Indiana. "Handsome" Harry Pierpont had failed to gain parole, even though his mother had approached Matt Leach of the Indiana State Police with a promise to deliver Dillinger to the lawman if Pierpont was released. Leach refused to honor the offer, which was undoubtedly phony.

Dillinger had plans to spring his friends out of prison. Flush with cash from the Indianapolis bank job, he first tried wrapping several guns in small packages covered with tar and sand. The bundles, which looked like stones, were thrown over the prison's walls. Although done at night and with the help of Harry Copeland, this stunt was quite risky for a man being hunted in several midwestern states. Discovered by another prisoner and turned in to the authorities, the guns never made their way to Pierpont and the others. Never one to give up, Dillinger hatched a plan to use a go-between who had access to the prison's shirt factory. Three guns were placed in a crate of thread and fabric to be smuggled behind bars. The weapons made it successfully inside the prison for use in the very near future.

On the personal side, romance again captured the attention
of the increasingly famous outlaw. Still smitten by the charms of
Mary Longnacker of Dayton, Ohio, Dillinger had been attempting
to communicate with her and she with him. With no permanent
address on his part, for obvious reasons, this was no easy task.
Finally, after successfully exchanging letters, a rendezvous was set.
The messages were intercepted, though, by the Dayton city police
and a trap was set at Longnacker's apartment house. Two detectives
were put on around-the-clock duty to watch the house, staying in
a room directly below Longnacker's. Amazingly, on the evening of
September 22, when Dillinger arrived in Dayton, the two policemen
had taken the night off. But Longnacker's landlady had remained
on watch and phoned the detectives when the love-struck outlaw

A guard stands watch at the Indiana State Prison in Michigan City.

arrived. A desk sergeant took the call and the landlady said, "He's here." The policeman on the phone replied, "Who's there?" She responded: "John Dillinger, you dumb flatfoot."

Within the hour the house was surrounded by police. The landlady knocked on the door and Longnacker, not expecting anything out of the ordinary, opened it. This time it was the police carrying powerful Thompson submachine guns. "Get'em up, John. We're the police!" they shouted. The couple had been looking at photographs of their World's Fair trip when the lawmen burst in. With hands raised Dillinger made a slight move which caused the detective to say, "Don't John. I'll kill you." Longnacker fainted, but quickly revived. The always well-armed Dillinger had two handguns on him, five in his suitcase, and one hidden in the couch.

Handcuffed and waiting to be taken off to jail, the unruffled Dillinger said, "When you fellows came in I didn't know if you were part of another gang or not. I know uniformed police, but not plainclothesmen. I thought you were somebody else." His car parked outside contained more guns, cash, and of course, the ever-present roofing nails. When surrounded by overwhelming firepower, Dillinger never tried to make an escape. That was the case here. Cool and composed he awaited what would happen to him next.

On a further search of Dillinger, police made an important discovery. They found a diagram that appeared to be a floor plan of the prison at Michigan City. The Dayton police immediately notified Leach. Upon arriving, Leach, in what was but another of his frequent mistakes, gave the document little credibility. Belittling the helpful detectives, Leach offhandedly remarked, "You've been reading too many detective novels. He ain't that big. They couldn't get out of there [Michigan City] if they tried." Leach met Dillinger for the first time and said to him, "Well, hotshot, how do you like my little surprise?" It was not really his surprise at all, as the Dayton police had captured Dillinger. During the questioning about a number of bank robberies, the only response from Dillinger was a crooked grin and the question, "What are you talking about?"

Other papers found on Dillinger included getaway maps used by the gang to elude police. These documents, not the prison breakout plan, were what Leach thought to be of most value. But he had been so disrespectful to the Dayton police that they did not give him the papers he wanted. The over-confident Leach was quickly proved wrong about which set of papers were more important. Four days later, on September 26, using the guns that Dillinger had paid for and secretly slipped into the prison's shirt factory, ten convicts broke out of the prison at Michigan City. Leach belatedly admitted that ten worse men to escape could not have been better selected if individually handpicked.

The escapees included several men who soon became Dillinger's partners in crime. Pierpont seems to have been the leader of the group that escaped. The others included John Hamilton, Charles Makley, and Russell Clark. The group actually escaped by walking out the prison's front door. Using the smuggled guns, they selectively took hostages, gaining access to room after room. Since prisoners were in the company of guards, the other guards on the walls saw nothing unusual. The band finally worked their way to the prison's main offices. A few of the guards were surprised by the prisoners' anger over their past treatment. One especially disliked guard was severely beaten. With only the front gate between them and freedom, one of the gang became either nervous or trigger happy and shot one of the prison employees in the side. But all ten of the men made it out and were free.

Outside the walls was a Chevrolet belonging to a sheriff who was delivering a new prisoner. Four of the men piled into that car, along with the sheriff as a hostage, and sped off. The other six men, including Pierpont, ran across the prison yard to a gas station and demanded the keys to the attendant's automobile. "Give us the keys to that car or I'll blow your brains out," yelled one of the escapees. The gas station attendant, evidently not scared by the gang, yelled back, "Go ahead, buddy!" and then took off running. Three shots were fired at him with one passing through his shirt, but he was unhurt. The six convicts finally commandeered a car from an elderly couple and drove away from Michigan City in a heavy rain.

The smaller group of four prisoners got their Chevrolet mired in the mud a few miles from the prison. Eventually, one of them was killed and the other three captured. The group of six, including Pierpont, had better luck. Zigzagging south across Indiana, they made it to Indianapolis. Before his own capture Dillinger had arranged for assistance when his friends arrived in the city. After changing clothes, the Pierpont party made their way to the Cincinnati, Ohio, area. Some of the men had girlfriends waiting for them on the outside and they, too, arrived at the hideout. Immediately they began planning to spring their rescuer, Dillinger, who was now behind bars in Ohio. There did seem to be loyalty among thieves.

Leach rushed to Michigan City. Listening to a commercial radio station, he heard what sounded like police sirens and gunshots. Thinking he was on the trail of a real crime, he arrived at a radio station that was broadcasting a play about a gunfight and robbery.

Leach, frustrated again, angrily arrested the radio station's director. Furious over the Michigan City breakout, Leach blamed others. First, he said the Dayton authorities had withheld the escape plan Dillinger had on him when arrested. This was not true. Leach next blamed the prison officials, noting, "Why for years it would have been possible to smuggle an elephant into the prison." Having made no friends in Michigan City, and with nothing else to do, he returned to Indianapolis empty-handed.

With Leach and other officials in Dayton, Dillinger hired a lawyer and then went uncharacteristically silent. Indiana governor Paul V. McNutt wanted the man whose parole he had signed back in Indiana. One veteran officer said he had the feeling that his prisoner had no worries. The reason was that Dillinger was fairly sure that a rescue party was on its way. While Dillinger was not a nationally known crime figure, there was the possibility that an attempt to liberate him might take place. Dayton lawmen took no chances, placing machine guns on the roofs of buildings surrounding the jail and doubling the night guard.

Harry Copeland, Dillinger's former Indiana partner, meanwhile had joined the Pierpont gang in Ohio. To release Dillinger, though, money would be needed. Amazingly the Terraplane car that Dillinger had signed over to his lawyer was now in Pierpont's possession. To obtain the cash they needed, Pierpont, Hamilton, and Clark robbed the bank in Saint Marys, Ohio, which also was Makley's hometown. The successful heist took place on October 3. Although the bank was officially closed, it was helping the U.S. mint distribute money to businesses. The robbery was called both quick and professional and yielded more than $14,000.

Meanwhile, in Dayton, the states of Indiana and Ohio were

wrangling over legal custody of Dillinger. Then, to the surprise
of most, he pleaded guilty to the Bluffton, Ohio, bank job. In late
September he was moved to the Allen County Jail in Lima, Ohio.
The crafty Dillinger no doubt knew that it would be much easier to
break out of the smaller Lima jail. From Lima he wrote to his father
in Mooresville. The letter read in part:

> Dear Dad,
>
> Hope this letter finds you well and not worrying too much over
> me. Maybe I'll learn someday Dad that you can't win in this
> game. I know I have been a big disappointment to you but I
> guess I did too much time, for where I went in a carefree boy
> I came out bitter toward everything in general. Of course Dad
> most of the blame lies with me for my environment was of the
> best but if I had gotten off more leniently when I made my first
> mistake this would never have happened. Dad don't believe all
> that the newspapers say about me for I am not guilty of half of
> the things I am charged with and I've never hurt anyone.
>
> From Johnnie

In spite of his limited education, Dillinger's letters, with the
occasional spelling or grammatical errors, were fairly well written.
Verbally articulate, he managed to convey his conversational
style to paper. He also wrote to his niece, Mary, while in the Lima
jail joking about being behind bars, possible weekend visits, and
chatting about baseball and the World Series. To her he also
maintained his innocence.

Longnacker, the female magnet that had drawn Dillinger to
Dayton, quickly dropped her jailed boyfriend. She resumed a
friendship with a man at her boardinghouse and soon married him.

Dillinger's girlfriend and companion, Evelyn "Billie" Frechette, in Chicago, 1936.

But Dillinger lost little sleep over his unreliable girfriend. Before landing in jail, he had apparently met another woman to whom he became strongly attached. Evelyn "Billie" Frechette had French and Native American ancestry and was born on the Menominee Indian Reservation in Wisconsin in 1907. She was five years younger than the thirty-year-old Dillinger. Photographs from the time probably do not do justice to her good looks. She was a little over five feet tall with black hair, brown eyes, and high cheekbones. Frechette had a checkered past with one son born out of wedlock in 1928 who died as an infant. A 1932 marriage ended ten days after the wedding, when her husband was sent to the federal penitentiary in Leavenworth, Kansas. Those who knew her said she was looking for thrills, could cuss like a sailor, and was tough as nails.

Women who were married to, lived with, or traveled with bank robbers and other outlaws were often referred to as "molls" by the press. The women's actions were often downplayed by the media or ignored all together. Their role has been described and explained better in recent times, especially by Ellen Poulsen in her book *Don't Call Us Molls: Women of the John Dillinger Gang*. In the volume's introduction William Helmer states that these women "prolonged the criminal careers of their boyfriends or husbands by renting apartments, buying cars, treating wounds, acting as couriers, and serving as camouflage."

There are a number of reasons these molls got involved with crooks. As with the outlaws themselves, some of it had to do with the times. Women rarely worked outside the home so their lives were often boring. Some, therefore, traveled with these men for sheer excitement. Most of these women had been in bad marriages, were often single or divorced, and worked at low-paying jobs.

Others, it has been suggested, came from abusive and neglectful homes or were naturally rebellious. And some of the females may actually have been in love. One federal official placed the role of molls on par with their male partners, viewing them as "more dangerous to society than the desperado himself. It is she and her kind who make him seek a life of crime." Part of the outrage was over the apparent light jail sentences—some as short as one day—given these women. As accomplices, it was thought, they deserved equal penalties under the law.

Mary Kinder, Pierpont's girlfriend, has been considered more than just a young woman in love or merely one out to have a good time. Joe Pinkston, curator of the John Dillinger Museum in Nashville, Indiana, wrote that Kinder "was a gang member. Unlike the other women, who were just girlfriends, Mary participated fully in the gang." This may be true to a certain extent. If she was never given full credit for her activities, it may be that she never walked into a bank with a Thompson submachine gun or drove a getaway car.

Frechette clearly met the definition of a moll. Dillinger had met her in Chicago. She was a hat-check girl and waitress among other professions. They had been introduced by Copeland, who knew Frechette through his girlfriend. When Frechette met Dillinger in Chicago she was working in a dancehall. Poulsen wrote that Dillinger was smitten by Frechette from the beginning. He was attracted, Poulsen said, to her "black, glistening eyes and haunted beauty." There was also her religious and cultural background. Dillinger, raised in a white, Midwest Protestant home was fascinated by Frechette's Roman Catholicism and Native American way of life.

Frechette was equally drawn to Dillinger. "I was twenty-five years old . . . and when I met John everything was changed," she said of their first meeting. "I started a new kind of life. He looked at me, smiled, and said, 'Where have you been all my life?' He treated me like a lady." Frechette later told *True Confessions* magazine that the night she met Dillinger she had not expected much more than a free drink and a dance. Instead she found romance. "There was something in those eyes that I will never forget," she wrote. "They were piercing and electric . . . with a carefree twinkle in them. They met my eyes and held me hypnotized. All I wanted to do was follow Dillinger."

At the time of Dillinger's capture in Dayton and captivity in Lima, Frechette was in Kokomo, Indiana. Somehow the love-struck Dillinger sent out word that he wanted her close by if he was able to escape. With his strong attraction to Frechette it is hard to guess why Dillinger was even visiting Longnacker in Dayton at the time of his capture. In any case Frechette, who was residing in a gambling house, was sent for by Pierpont.

While Dillinger's romantic business was being handled, work was proceeding on making his escape a reality. The Pierpont gang's first idea was to bribe Sheriff Jess Sarber of Lima, Ohio, through a lawyer. They quickly found that the lawman could not be bought. Therefore, the job would have to be done the hard way. On October 11 Pierpont, Clark, Makley, Hamilton, and a fifth man, Edward Shouse, drove two cars, one of them Dillinger's Terraplane, into Lima to "case" the town. Pierpont, always a bit rash and ready for action, suggested they storm the jail to free Dillinger. Cooler heads prevailed. More information was needed and it was suggested one of the molls pretend to be Dillinger's sister in order to survey the layout inside of the jail. That idea was never carried out.

On Columbus Day, October 12, the five men returned to Lima.

Imitating a bank robbery plan, Pierpont, Clark, and Makley went inside the jail; Shouse served as a lookout; and Hamilton stayed with the two getaway cars. Sarber, his wife Lucy, and a deputy were sitting in the jail's office. It was 6:30 in the evening and supper for the inmates had just finished. Neither Sarber nor the deputy had on their sidearms. Referring to Dillinger as a "punk," the sheriff had not taken seriously the potential danger his prisoner represented. When the three men strode into the jail they told the sheriff they were from Michigan City to transport Dillinger back to the prison. Sarber asked the men for papers or some kind of identification. It was at that point things went out of control.

Pulling his gun Pierpont replied, "Here's our credentials." Sarber replied, "You can't do that," and before ending his sentence reached for a gun in his desk drawer. Pierpont responded by shooting the sheriff twice in the side, seriously wounding him. Clark's gun then accidently went off nicking his own finger. Makley brutally struck the wounded sheriff with the butt of his gun, causing it to fire. With all the gunplay the sheriff's unarmed deputy decided not to move. Pierpont fired more bullets into the air and then struck the incapacitated sheriff again. He was ready to deliver another blow when Lucy retrieved the keys to the jail cells.

Dillinger heard the gunshots while he was playing cards in the cellblock. He calmly picked up his coat seeming to know the ruckus going on in the office meant his friends had arrived for him. Dillinger even offered to take a fellow prisoner with him. The man refused, but shook hands with his new friend. Shooting wildly to keep the other prisoners away, Pierpont brought Dillinger out from the cells. Seeing the sheriff lying in blood on the floor appeared to deeply disturb Dillinger. The violence brought strong criticism from him, but the disapproval fell on deaf ears. With Sarber mortally wounded the heartless Pierpont then locked Lucy and the deputy in a cell. They were not even allowed to call a physician.

The gang's getaway went unnoticed. When aid finally arrived for the wounded sheriff, it was too late. Sarber died at 8:00 p.m. at the hospital. The outraged citizens of Lima formed six posses to chase Dillinger and his confederates, but they had disappeared. Upon hearing about the jailbreak in Lima, Indiana officials raided the Dillinger farm in Mooresville. For the next year John Sr.'s place would be closely watched. What law officials observed was the honest farmer shucking corn and cutting wood.

Violence, of the most serious nature, had entered Dillinger's world. There had been fistfights in the early robberies and then the gun that failed to go off while aimed at the bank employee in Rockville, Indiana, but a dead sheriff was different. Attention now rapidly centered on Dillinger and his accomplices. Newspapers did not have to wait long for the Dillinger story to continue. Cooling their heels for only two days, the gang made another daring raid, this time in Indiana.

To continue their crime spree the gang needed larger and more powerful weapons. While automatic weapons could be purchased easier than handguns, this was not an option. The gang was becoming too well-known to openly buy weapons. On the evening of October 14 the trio of Dillinger, Pierpont, and Makley entered the Auburn, Indiana, police station, surprising two officers. "Have you got any guns?" they asked. An honest "yes" was the reply. The arsenal taken consisted of two Thompson submachine guns, an array of revolvers and automatic pistols, three much-needed bulletproof vests, and a sizable supply of ammunition. To add insult to injury Leach misunderstood a tip on the heist and was waiting for the gang in Aurora, not Auburn.

McNutt took the crime outbreak quite seriously. The silver-haired governor had gotten involved in the Dayton arrest and legal wrangling by signing extradition papers for Dillinger. McNutt directed Leach to form a special squad of six lawmen in his state with the sole purpose of tracking down Dillinger and his associates. He also increased the security of armories in the state with seven hundred members of the Indiana National Guard and considered using airplanes, tanks, and even poison gas. Ironically, McNutt was also from Mooresville, the now high-profile bank robber's adopted hometown. While McNutt's biographer never mentions Dillinger's name, it has been suggested that the governor, who had presidential ambitions, was hurt politically by his fellow Hoosier's crime spree.

The equally humiliated Leach upped the ante by overstating the number of Dillinger-related robberies and exaggerating his adversary by calling him "more deadly than Machine Gun Kelly." Leach also attempted to use psychological tricks by implying that Dillinger was the head of the gang rather than Pierpont, hoping to cause dissension between the two men. The idea did not work. While the gang always followed their exploits in the newspapers, leadership seemed not to matter to either man. Whether the leader or not, Dillinger soon became better known than Pierpont or his others partners in crime.

One of the newspapers that Dillinger no doubt read was the *Mooresville Times*, which wrote on October 19, 1933: "John W. Dillinger . . . liberated last week from the Lima, Ohio jail at the cost of a sheriff's life, would never have figured in major crimes

In addition to his service as Indiana governor, Paul V. McNutt had a distinguished career as U.S. High Commissioner to the Philippines, head of the Federal Security Agency, and chairman of the War Manpower Commission during World War II.

had the judge who sentenced him for the first offense been more lenient." This was to be an oft-repeated theme by many, including John Sr. The elder Dillinger was frequently and accurately portrayed with sympathy as a humble man of the land working hard on his Mooresville farm. If John Sr.'s son was causing trouble, to the citizens of their hometown it did not seem to be the fault of either man.

The very next day after an apologetic piece appeared in the newspaper, Dillinger and Pierpont struck the Peru, Indiana, police station. (Dillinger and his former prison friend Homer Van Meter had actually visited the Peru police station earlier pretending to be tourists and had been given a full tour of the facility.) They made off with two more machine guns, numerous handguns and bulletproof vests, and a tear-gas gun. Oddly handcuffs and police badges were also taken. Dillinger passed on stealing a cabinet of liquor, telling one of the officers "I don't drink." In comparison, Pierpont kept up his tough-guy image, telling the Peru officers "I haven't killed anybody for a week and I'd just as soon shoot one of you as not. Go ahead and get funny." No one got "funny," and the pair drove off in the Terraplane. The boldness of hitting a second police station within a week only added to the gang's notoriety.

Always responding to the last incident, jails in Indiana began to bolster their defenses. In Fort Wayne and Indianapolis steel-plated cages were built inside the jails for added protection. Metal bars were placed in police station windows. Indianapolis purchased armored cars mounted with machine guns. In Marion fifty firemen were armed and sworn in as special police officers. Jack Edwards, the city's mayor, asked the board of public works for permission to turn the police station into a fort. Towns requested state funds for two-way radios. The National Guard offered its services while the

American Legion volunteered its members for vigilante service.

Banks, too, had decided to add steel cages and place guards inside them to enhance their defenses. One of these cages had been placed in the Central National Bank of Greencastle, Indiana, where the gang struck next. On Monday, October 23, Dillinger, Pierpont, and Makley strolled into the bank while Clark stood guard outside. Timing was everything, so Makley carried a stopwatch. The security man, who was supposed to be in the steel cage, had left to tend to the furnace in the basement. Pierpont used the ploy of asking a teller to change a twenty-dollar bill. He then quickly got down to business, displaying a machine gun followed by the now familiar statement, "This is a holdup." Dillinger took the equally familiar and now trademark leap over a railing landing behind the counter. Pierpont merely opened a gate and walked into the same area. Dillinger smashed his way into the cashier's cage and the two men began sweeping bills and coins, even the heavy silver dollars and half dollars, into a bag.

Once a robbery began events often took unpredictable twists and turns. A robbery is something citizens during the Great Depression knew could happen, but were genuinely surprised when it did. A person can never know how they will react when faced with a tough guy holding a machine gun. For example, on this day a bank employee slipped out the back door and began looking for nails to place under the getaway car. By doing this, the man failed to contact the sheriff's office that was directly across the street. If he would have, a well-armed contingent of deputies on duty, along with a visiting state policeman, might have stopped the robbery.

When Dillinger saw a farmer standing by a counter with some change laying on it, he asked, "Is that your money or the bank's?"

"Mine," the farmer answered. "Keep it," replied Dillinger, "We only want the bank's." Clark, the outside man, was busy keeping gawkers at bay and yet the growing crowd failed to capture the attention of the lawmen sitting across the street. Makley's stopwatch had ticked off five minutes since the robbery had begun and it was time to go. Clark collected the gang members in the getaway car. Before he left the increasingly arrogant Dillinger quipped to customers, "Boys, take a good look so you will be sure to know me the next time you see me." He then jumped into the car and the gang was gone. The state police were notified and roadblocks were set up at nearby communities, but the getaway car was never seen. Apparently confident, the gang took time to stop and fill the car's gas tank a few miles outside of town before heading west to Terre Haute.

Citizens were actually delighted that the band of robbers had their money and were gone with no one hurt. Oddly, the Greencastle bankers showed little concern about the robbery. Equally peculiar was the differing amounts of money reported stolen. The estimated $75,000 in bonds and cash was probably the gang's biggest take yet. Thus began the suspicion of cooperation and deals between the robbers and the banks.

The Banking Act of 1933, part of Franklin D. Roosevelt's New Deal program, protected depositors, not banks. Banks were only protected from theft if they had private insurance, which the Greencastle bank did have. Since many banks were failing at this time, a robbery that took place with an unknown amount of money stolen, or an incorrect amount reported to the authorities, was not always an unwelcome event. Which bank jobs by Dillinger were "setups" has never been established, but vague statements as to the exact amount stolen, such as the one made by the bank president in

Greencastle, were suspicious. "We are not seeking any publicity in connection with our experience with Mr. Dillinger," he stated.

Believing Indiana authorities unable to handle the ever-growing problem of bank robberies in its state, the *Indianapolis Times* made a plea for help to U.S. Attorney General Homer Cummings. The *Indianapolis News* printed an editorial cartoon showing outlaws chasing lawmen out of the state. Federal authorities were already beginning to take notice of the situation in the Midwest. In fact, a federal agency seemed ready, and at times willing, to take on the assignment. The Bureau (sometimes referred to as Division) of Investigation had been created in 1908 as an arm of the Justice Department. President Theodore Roosevelt, a former president of the New York City Board of Police Commissioners, had recommended the department, but Congress, fearing a national police force, vetoed it. Not to be stopped, Roosevelt located a "special fund" and quietly hired thirty-four agents for his new Bureau.

While having no charter, the Bureau's charge was to gather facts and evidence on interstate crimes. The Bureau became active in the post-World War I period pursuing Communists, both real and imagined, by then President Woodrow Wilson's Attorney General A. Mitchell Palmer. In July 1935 the name of the organization was changed to the Federal Bureau of Investigation.

In 1924 when the Red Scare had diminished, twenty-nine-year-old J. Edgar Hoover became the Bureau's director. A native of Washington, D.C., then a very southern city, he was a lawyer and graduate of George Washington University. Surrounding himself with other southerners, Hoover chose young, white men who held law degrees and came from traditional families. African Americans did not become bona fide, working agents until the 1960s and there

Homer Cummings, U.S. Attorney General, leaves the White House after a January 21, 1935, conference on legislative matters with President Franklin D. Roosevelt.

was only one Jew in the ranks of agents for years. After Hoover's death in 1972 the FBI became a more diverse organization.

By 1933 Hoover and his small Bureau had begun to track the nation's outlaws. The director's aim was to build a new kind of law enforcement entity in the United States. A positive image in the eyes of the public was critical for the Bureau. Therefore, Hoover was careful not to have the Bureau become too involved in any case unless the chances for success were above average. As for Dillinger, Hoover did give limited approval to the Bureau's Cincinnati field office to offer assistance to the Indiana police. Across the country there were twenty-five special agents in charge who headed up

LIBRARY OF CONGRESS

A 1924 photograph of J. Edgar Hoover at his desk during his days as acting director of the Bureau of Investigation, later known as the Federal Bureau of Investigation.

the field offices. The outbreak of bank robberies and kidnappings that took place in the early 1930s was not actually a national phenomenon. Most of the action took place in the heartland of the United States, from Minnesota and the Dakotas south to Texas and from Ohio west to Iowa.

With armed bands of citizens and law enforcement personnel roaming the state, the common man on the street was left to wonder. The bad guys did seem to be in control. Back in Indiana Leach was trying everything to bring some semblance of order to the situation. To his embarrassment it became known that someone had sent him an 1896 book titled *How to Be a Detective*. Many thought it had been sent by Dillinger, but the hoax had actually been played on Leach by two newspapermen. Those in charge of protecting the public seemed to have run out of ideas. Merely setting up roadblocks and chasing the robbers after they had stolen the money was not working. For Leach there seemed only one thing left to do. As October 1933 drew to a close and the Dillinger gang remained on the loose, Leach canceled Halloween in the Hoosier State.

4

Chicago

The public was of two minds about the ruckus being raised by
John Dillinger. Although the death of the sheriff in Lima, Ohio, had
happened quite recently, the event seemed to have been forgotten.
The idea was developing that Dillinger might actually be a kind of
Robin Hood—robbing from the rich and giving to the poor. Not
that he gave what he stole to the poor. But his escapes, close calls,
and gentlemanly behavior were all giving the outlaw a celebrity-like
reputation. Part of the myth was centered on the public's dislike of
banks. In the midst of the Great Depression, with unemployment
high and poverty the rule for most Americans, bankers were
unpopular. Personal savings had been lost and many blamed banks
for foreclosing on homes and farms. If Dillinger was sticking his
finger in the eye of the bankers, then, some thought, good for him.

This is evident in the newspapers of the day. One citizen wrote:
"I am for John Dillinger. Not that I am upholding him in any of his
crimes; that is, if he did any. Why should the law have wanted John
Dillinger for bank robbery? He wasn't any worse than bankers and
politicians who took the poor people's money. Dillinger did not rob
poor people. He robbed those who became rich by robbing the poor.
I am for Johnnie." Another person wrote, "He [Dillinger] isn't half
as cheap as a crooked banker or a crooked politician because he did

Chicago crime boss Al Capone, known by the nickname Scarface, was convicted of income tax evasion in 1931 and spent eight years in prison before being paroled. He died on January 21, 1947.

give the bankers a chance to fight, and they never gave the people a chance." Although Dillinger and his partners were being called the Terror Gang, robbing banks seemed alright with the public as long as no lives were lost. One writer called this response to Dillinger's activities "misplaced admiration."

While only a few men and women ever came into personal contact with Dillinger, there was sympathy for him. Even those close to him made excuses for Dillinger. A gang moll once said, "Johnnie's just an ordinary fellow. Of course he goes out and holds up banks and things, but he's really just like any other fellow, aside from that." But there was also fear. Some policemen would go out of their way in order not to confront the gang. When told that a holdup by the Dillinger gang was in progress less than two blocks away, a patrolman replied, "I don't care. I ain't on duty."

There was a difference between being a gangster or racketeer and the crimes being carried out by Dillinger during this time. The term "gangster" came about in 1896 and in general referred simply to a member of a gang. The term "racketeer" has also been used when speaking of those involved in illegal activity. But the terms gangster and racketeer most often referred to organized crime and men such as Al Capone, Dutch Schultz, and Bugsy Siegel. These men were involved in gambling, extortion, and bootlegging during Prohibition. Dillinger, the Ma Barker Gang, Baby Face Nelson, and others were usually bank robbers with an occasional kidnapping thrown in. Dillinger himself never engaged in kidnapping.

It was late October 1933 and the Dillinger Gang was nowhere to be found. Although new precautions were put in place by law enforcement officials, the gang continued to elude the authorities. Roadblocks appeared to be useless against the gang. Handsome

Harry Pierpont commented, probably in exaggeration, that he had passed through thirty of them undetected. In late October, looking for even more weaponry, Dillinger and two associates may have cased Fort Benjamin Harrison, an U.S. Army Reserve base near Indianapolis. They supposedly said they were rug salesmen and talked to both the base commander and chaplain. (Gang members cased one bank posing as journalists). Dillinger also visited his sister, her husband, and his niece in Indianapolis without detection.

The gang was actually spending little time in either Indiana or Ohio. Dillinger and his companions had moved to Chicago. With their molls, the group decided that the Windy City was the safest place to hide. Chicago had a reputation for crime and corruption. They also could easily fence (sell) stolen bonds and jewels, buy protection, and make connections with other crooks. Lost among the population of a large city, their increasingly lavish lifestyle stood out less. They dressed well, lived in comfortable apartments, and often ate at first-class restaurants, where beer and frog legs were a Dillinger favorite. For entertainment they attended sporting events, movies, and drove their new automobiles. While the women drank hard liquor, the men preferred beer.

Mary Kinder, girlfriend of one of the gang members, gave this description of their life in Chicago: "We'd all go to dances, taverns, restaurants, and prizefights. Nobody hid around. We'd read different stuff, listened to the radio and everything. Nobody was boss. They'd sit down and talk things over, and when they got money they'd count it, then divide it between them. There wasn't no boss at all. Everyone tries to say Harry [Pierpont] was so mean and Dillinger was boss, but there wasn't no boss or nothing like that." The men and their molls often shared an apartment and at times things got tense. Billie Frechette, Dillinger's girlfriend, did not like to cook, which caused discord among the other women who took turns in the kitchen. Dillinger at one point had to tell Frechette that she needed to help. The independent Frechette assisted a bit more after this dispute, but not much.

There was always the danger of capture, even in Chicago. Unknowingly, Dillinger and his friends had taken an informant into their confidence. Arthur "Art" McGinnis began working for private detectives hired by banks, who were in turn working with the police. McGinnis wished to capture the entire gang because he would receive a percentage on all that had been stolen, not just Dillinger's cut of the robberies. Therefore, he kept some information secret, even from his employers. Fearful of capture, Pierpont was the most cautious of the gang, knowing that their photographs were appearing with greater frequency in newspapers. Handsome Harry was right to be worried.

Although they had captured each gang member at one time or another, local and state police did not seem a real threat to the increasingly confident Dillinger. In 1933 there was no national police force other than the developing Bureau. The new president, Franklin D. Roosevelt, at first had little interest in such an organization. Keeping banks open was higher on the president's agenda than keeping them from being robbed. But events would place the Bureau in the midst of the fight against the crime spree taking place in the Midwest.

In his book *Public Enemies: America's Greatest Crime Wave and the Birth of the FBI, 1933–34*, Bryan Burrough maintains that the crime war began with the Kansas City Massacre in June 1933. The bloodbath at the city's train station was an attempt by outlaws

to free a prisoner being taken from Hot Springs, Arkansas, to the
federal penitentiary in Leavenworth, Kansas. In the shootout
the prisoner, Frank "Jelly" Nash, was killed along with three local
policemen and a Bureau agent. It was later discovered that Charles
"Pretty Boy" Floyd had been one of the shooters. The Kansas City
killings pulled the Bureau into the crime war. However, with only
250 special agents and sixty accountants the Bureau's duties mainly
involved collecting information. Its agents had no authority to
arrest suspects, let alone carry weapons. Most, in fact, had never
fired a gun. As he pushed for legislation to expand the Bureau's
authority, J. Edgar Hoover decided that Dillinger was now a high-
profile crook and worthy of his time. Always politically astute,
Hoover was careful in his pursuit of Dillinger. He wanted to avoid
having his agents blamed for mistakes, while looking for ways to
take credit for any successes.

Although yet to be captured, Pierpont and four other men were
indicted in Ohio for the murder of the Lima sheriff. Because of the
killing, Pierpont was viewed as a man out of control, but Dillinger
was not always the easy-going gentleman outlaw portrayed in
the press. He also had his dark side that often included plans
for retaliation. The reason he had visited the military fort in
Indianapolis was to secure heavy weapons for a possible assault on
the Pendleton Reformatory in Indiana, the place Dillinger still held
a grudge against because of his mistreatment by prison guards. He
also left Chicago for a trip to Dayton, Ohio, to track down the two
detectives who had captured him in that city. The arrest there still
bothered him. That expedition came to nothing.

While Dillinger and Frechette were enjoying the Chicago social
life, authorities were aware of his presence. A special "Dillinger

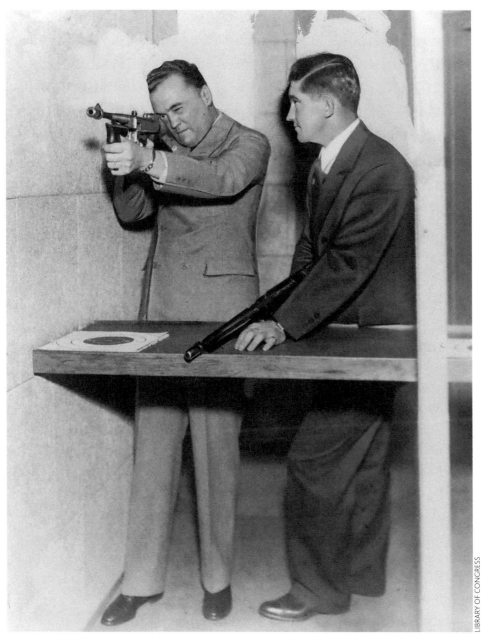

In a staged publicity photograph, Hoover shows Detroit Tigers manager Mickey Cochrane how to fire a Thompson submachine gun at the U.S. Department of Justice in Washington, D.C., in September 1935.

Squad" or "Secret Squad" was established by the Chicago Police Department in late 1933 to pursue the Hoosier outlaw. McGinnis continued to feed information to law officials while maintaining that Dillinger be taken with his gang, not alone. The chance to take him alone occurred early on the evening of November 15, 1933. Dillinger had a case of "barber's itch," a rashlike condition of the scalp that may have been ringworm. He was being treated by a dermatologist, Doctor Charles Eye, whose office was on Irving Park Boulevard. With knowledge of this appointment the Chicago police set a trap.

Hearing of the plot, Matt Leach had arrived in Chicago and convinced local authorities that Indiana had a stake in Dillinger's capture. True to form, Leach's presence seemed to jinx the situation. Forrest Huntington, the private investigator to whom McGinnis was reporting, later told what happened that November evening

> We met the squads [Chicago police and Indiana State Police] about three squares from the doctor's office. We waited until 7:25 p.m. when Dillinger and his girl, Evelyn Frechette, drove up in the Essex Terraplane. He parked his car facing South on Keeler Avenue, alighted, crossed the street and entered the doctor's office upstairs. The girl remained in the car. The two squad cars pulled down immediately in front of Dillinger's car and parked less than seventy-five feet away from the Terraplane. A few moments later we observed Dillinger leave the doctor's office, get in his car and start backing into Irving Boulevard! We started after him at once, passed the two police squad cars, and caught up with Dillinger's car about two squares east. We pulled alongside the left side of his speeding machine and an Indiana State Police officer fired five loads of buckshot into the left door of the Terraplane, as well as

the window and front tire. But Dillinger kept going. Officers
Rooney and Artery also fired their revolvers into Dillinger's car
. . . travelling at a speed of about sixty miles per hour.

Backing his Terraplane up and heading in the opposite direction
after leaving the doctor's office was again a case of the "Dillinger
Luck." Neither he nor Frechette seemed to have noticed that they
were in the middle of a police trap. Although Dillinger could drive
almost as fast in reverse as forward, this move seems to have
happened purely by chance. The lawmen were taken totally by
surprise when their target drove off in the opposite direction. A
great deal of firepower was directed at the Terraplane, but there was
no return fire. Dillinger was focused on his steering and locating a
way to escape. The chase through the city streets went on for five
miles with speeds of up to seventy-five miles per hour. Dillinger
ducked into an alley and turned off his lights, and the police sped
by without noticing the Terraplane. One of the policemen involved
in the chase later said of Dillinger, "That bird can sure drive."

After the chase, the police thought that Dillinger had been
shooting at them from a secret window in the car. Police also
said that the Terraplane was armor plated. It was not. They later
discovered that the bullet holes in their vehicles were from their
own guns. The lawmen had purposely tried not to shoot directly
at Dillinger, fearing they would kill him, sending the Terraplane
swerving into their squad car. The next day police found the
Terraplane abandoned on the far north side of Chicago. There were
twenty-two bullet holes in it, which makes what one lawman said
ring true, "I missed that rat by an inch."

The wild car chase had one other result. McGinnis was identified
by the gang as the informant, thus causing the police to lose their

only "inside man." More important, the Dillinger gang went deeper underground, using backup hideouts and finally becoming more careful. This did not stop them from staging what Robert Cromie and Joseph Pinkston, authors of *Dillinger: A Short and Violent Life*, have called one of the gang's "most spectacular" bank raids more than a hundred miles north of Chicago in Racine, Wisconsin.

The November 20 robbery of the American Bank and Trust Company of Racine was extremely well-planned, with the gang returning to their customary methods of operation. The details of the robbery, from dialogue to actions, were classic and often repeated in crime movies of the time. Much of the information on the gang's mode of operation may have come from McGinnis. According to the informant the success of Dillinger, Pierpont, and their associates could be attributed to planning. In spite of Leach's attempt to divide the gang over the leadership issue, it was learned that Dillinger and Pierpont were actually coleaders. They did most of the planning, gave the orders, and apparently trusted only each other. What could be considered the original Dillinger Gang was composed of Pierpont, Charles Makley, Russell Clark, and Homer Van Meter. This group held together for only about three months, from October 1933 until late January 1934.

The gang's holdup routine followed the pattern of scouting the bank for several days before deciding to rob it. Rough drawings of the bank floor plans were then made. The number of customers and employees that might be expected was noted. Painstaking getaway plans were formed and plotted in great detail for both time and distance. To draw the least amount of attention after the bank had been hit, the gang drove under the speed limit unless being pursued.

Unfortunately, most of this inside information from McGinnis came after the Racine robbery. Leaving the getaway driver outside, four men entered the bank in Racine on that Monday afternoon in late November. The group consisted of Dillinger, Pierpont, Makley, and Clark. Van Meter drove a new Buick with flashy yellow wire wheels. Under their overcoats the well-dressed foursome hid their Thompson submachine guns. One of the gang pasted two Red Cross posters across the bank windows, preventing passersby from seeing what was taking place. When the posters were in place the bandits gave the standard order of "Stick 'em up!"

As Dillinger went behind the cages (apparently not jumping over them this time), Makley said again "Stick 'em up!" At that point, according to a teller named Harold Graham, things began to go haywire. "I thought some darned fool wanted me to wait on him," Graham said later, "and because there was a lot of currency there it was not too unusual for someone to make a crack like that. I thought, 'Oh, you darned fool, go down to the next window and get waited on!'" Makley, thinking he was either being ignored or disobeyed, let go with a single shot from the Thompson. "As I turned, he caught me with a shot that went through my arm and into my side just below the right elbow, cutting the top off my right hip," Graham recalled. "When I fell to the floor I thought, 'My God, it's a holdup!'"

Graham was able to hit the alarm, which rang both inside and outside the bank. Upon hearing the clanging bells Dillinger and Pierpont came from the back of the bank. One of the men, probably Pierpont, kicked the wounded Graham in the side for punching the alarm. The two robbers then began to empty the cash drawers. The persistent Graham then hit another button, a silent one, which notified the Racine police. Dillinger, cool under pressure as usual, took his time as he worked with the bank president to open the vault. While he may have been calm, mayhem ruled. Men and women ducked under desks and hid in closets and backrooms. One man sat perfectly still in the safe deposit box room. Another fellow tried to escape out the backdoor only to run into the getaway car and its driver. He beat a hasty retreat back inside the bank. The fear was real. Said one man later, "When you look down the barrel end of a .45 it looks like a cannon."

The police finally arrived after first not taking the situation seriously, thinking it was a false alarm. This often happened during bank robberies. Doing so was a big mistake. The first officer to enter was quickly disarmed. The second, carrying a Thompson himself to match the robbers' firepower, was shot twice by Makley, who then took the machine gun and shot out the windows of the bank, splattering the onlookers outside with glass. While all this was taking place, Dillinger and Pierpont continued in their business-like way to empty the bank's vault. When one employee pleaded, "For God's sake, mister, point that gun the other way!," Pierpont laughed and said, "As long as you're a good boy you don't have to worry." When a third policeman walked in, Dillinger wisecracked, "Come right in and join us."

Although Dillinger and Pierpont left with about $28,000, they had missed $50,000 in large bills in one of the teller's drawers. It looked like the gang was going to have to shoot its way out—police were waiting for them outside in addition to a crowd of almost a hundred. Instead they decided to use hostages to move safely to their getaway car. Makley sprayed more bullets from his Thompson above the crowd and then toward some men he took for policemen. Some stray bullets came close to several individuals, but no one on the sidewalks was hurt. The hostages were bank president Grover Weyland, a police officer, and three women. Using the group as a human shield, the bank robbers moved to their getaway car. The ploy worked with some of the hostages inside the car and some standing on the running boards. Police and citizens both aimed their guns at the car, but firing was just too dangerous.

Few details as to what occurred after the robberies are known. But there was as much planning for the getaway as there was for the robbery. In the case of the Racine robbery, the hostages made excellent witnesses. Before leaving the bank, Weyland had been struck across the face for making a smart remark to one of the robbers. While in the car, Weyland was berated by Makley for filling the bags with one-dollar bills. "Just keep counting," the bank president lied, "You took all we had."

As they drove away from Racine, Makley began using some obscene language. Pierpont said, "Cut it out, Mac, we got a lady in the car." One hostage was held by the belt of his pants to keep him from falling off the running board of the car. The hostages were let off along the roads one at a time as the gang moved farther and farther away from the scene of the crime. The policeman was the first to be dropped off, thinking he surely would be shot. "It all looked like a movie," he later said. The gang on this job stopped to change license plates, but not cars. This was peculiar due to the fact that the large black Buick was easy to identify because of its yellow wheels. Makley was keeping track of the mileage on the getaway map. At one point the auto stopped. The gang retrieved a hidden gas can and refilled the nearly empty tank.

Eventually down to two hostages, Weyland and bank teller Ursula Patzke, the mood of the gang seemed to lighten. "Maybe we ought to take you along. Can you cook?" Dillinger asked Patzke. "After a fashion," she cautiously replied. Things tensed slightly when a funeral procession approached. Farther down the road there was a farm auction. The numerous automobiles along the side of the road gave the gang pause. But inside the getaway car Pierpont became surprisingly friendly. He offered the freezing Patzke his coat and gave the bald banker his hat. Dillinger even waved to a farmer in a field yelling, "Hi, Joe."

Thirty-five miles outside of Racine, the Buick pulled over and Weyland (minus Pierpont's hat) and Patzke were tied with shoelaces to a tree, facing each other. The two were told to wait ten minutes before leaving. Easily releasing themselves, they were finally given a ride back to Racine by a farmer working in a nearby field. Since they wore no masks, the gang was easily identified. Weyland was later asked what Dillinger was like. "Genial," he answered. The Racine robbery and the friendly and gracious behavior of Dillinger only added to his growing reputation.

After dividing the money, the gang again went into hiding. Dillinger bought a new Terraplane for eight hundred dollars after the Racine job. Deciding to split up, Pierpont and his girlfriend went to Houston, Texas, while Dillinger and Frechette took a vacation in the resort town of Hot Springs, Arkansas. After this brief break, Dillinger returned to Chicago. He should have stayed longer in Arkansas. Things continued to be "hot" for him as the police were increasingly able to locate his hideouts, back-up hideouts, and back-up, back-up hideouts. The attention he was drawing caused Hoover to decide to brand Dillinger as "The Number One Criminal at Large." Chicago and Indiana went with the title "Public Enemy Number One," which Hoover later borrowed. The Chicago gangster and bootlegger, Al Capone, had held the title in 1931.

On December 28, 1933, the state of Illinois posted a list of twenty-one "public enemies." Dillinger was number one followed by four male members of his various gangs with Pierpont, Hamilton, and Makley being the next three. Van Meter was number eighteen. Two Dillinger gang molls, Pearl Elliot and Kinder, were numbers eight and nine on the list. Lester Gillis (aka Baby Face Nelson) was twenty-one, which no doubt made him unhappy for two reasons— he was not higher on the list and they had again referred to him as "Baby Face." At this point, though, Nelson was not connected with Dillinger.

Dillinger was often blamed for killings and other robberies whenever his associates were involved. John Hamilton was an escapee of the Michigan City breakout and possibly one of the Racine robbers. On December 14 he engaged in a shootout in a Chicago garage with a policeman. Hamilton killed the officer and then made his getaway, leaving his girlfriend behind. The abandoned woman said she did not know Hamilton and was freed. Five days later, Ed Shouse, another Dillinger crony who had been booted out of the gang, also found himself in major trouble. On December 19 Shouse had been involved in a shootout in Paris, Illinois, where a policeman was accidently killed by one of his own partners. Shouse was captured and began to tell authorities what he knew about Dillinger's activities. What he told them only added to the Dillinger myth. Shouse, who was questioned by state police, said in his opinion Dillinger and his men were "daring and desperate." He told the lawman that they had little chance of capturing the gang as they had sworn never to be taken alive.

A December 13, 1933, Chicago robbery has also been attributed to Dillinger. He, along with Makley, Pierpont, and Hamilton, allegedly hit the Chicago Unity Trust and Savings for $220,000. Due to the large amount of money (it would have been their largest robbery to date), the report was no doubt false. It demonstrated, though, that Dillinger and his men were not the only gang working at the time.

The Chicago police upped their commitment to the Dillinger unit by hiring a policeman with a record of killing a dozen crooks. As a result, in late December a police raid at a mistaken address ended with three men dead. The "Dillinger Squad" found that the men had no connection at all with the Indiana bandit. It had been a case of shooting first and asking questions later. In a separate episode two other men, not connected to Dillinger, were also shot. With all this random gunplay taking place, Dillinger and several members of his gang decided to take a long vacation to a warmer and hopefully safer climate. On December 14, 1933, three vehicles carrying five men and four women departed freezing Chicago for sunny Florida.

5

Laying Low in the Sun

The exact number of cars and occupants that left Chicago in December 1933 varies depending on who told the story. Most are fairly certain that John Dillinger and Billie Frechette drove to Florida along with Harry Pierpont and his girlfriend, Mary Kinder. Russell Clark and his wife, Bernice; her sister, Pat Cherrington; Charles Makley; and Homer Van Meter were also on this road trip. John Hamilton, who had recently killed a Chicago policeman, may have later joined the group. Dillinger visited his sister, half-brother, and other relatives in Indiana on his way to Florida, leaving Christmas presents for the family.

Sometime between December 19 and 21 the gang arrived in Daytona Beach, Florida, driving their new vehicles—a Terraplane, a Studebaker, and one of the speedy V-8 Fords. They split up, staying in luxurious beach homes, fancy apartments, and hotels. One of the homes, a mansion, had four fireplaces. The plan was to stay for three or four months. Even this far away from the Midwest there were constant worries about being recognized. Two days after their arrival, Pierpont and his girlfriend found their hotel swarming with police. The lawmen were there to investigate the suicide of another guest. The local police had heard "gangsters" might be in the state. This information came from Matt Leach of the Indiana State Police.

He had a report that his quarry was in Miami, a five-hour drive to the south.

In his novel *Handsome Harry*, a fictional tale with Pierpont as the narrator, writer James Carlos Blake described what the Florida vacation might have been like for the Dillinger gang. Blake tells of the group seeing the ocean for the first time and buying sunglasses, bathing suits, and suntan lotion just like any other tourists on their first visit to the South. "We spent the mornings walking on the beach, lazing on the sundeck, and watching the pelicans dive for fish," Pierpont notes in the book. They ate lunch every day at a diner called the Mermaid and then went Christmas shopping.

After the clashes, gunplay, and robberies over the past six months, this vacation in the sun must have seemed delightful to the group. While always on the lookout for trouble, they managed to relax and have some fun. There was swimming, fishing, endless card playing, and a trip to Miami to see airplane races, in spite of authorities looking for them there. The gang always read the newspapers, following their real and imaginary actions. They continued to be blamed (or given credit) for robberies in states that they were nowhere near. Dillinger read one day that he had shot a dog in Chicago. "That's going too far. How could I hit a dog in Chicago from way down here in Florida? I wonder if the dog's name was Matt [Leach]," he said.

On Christmas Day, expensive gifts were exchanged among the men and their molls. Pierpont bought a new car in Jacksonville, north of Daytona Beach, and sent his girlfriend to get it. The unattached Makley had picked up a girlfriend during his short time in Florida. Frechette received jewelry and a puppy from Dillinger. But all this happiness was not to last. The couple had either a mild quarrel or genuine physical skirmish, which it actually was is unknown. Dillinger gave Frechette the Terraplane and sent her back to the Indian reservation in Wisconsin. Since she later met up with the gang in January, it may have been merely a case of a brief falling out between the two.

New Year's Eve brought out the apparent pent-up energy in the group. After seeing a few movies they decided to celebrate by getting out their Thompsons and shooting into the air over the Atlantic Ocean. Neighbors in Daytona Beach finally began to wonder about this well-dressed, apparently wealthy group spending so much time in their town. Later, after the gang had left Florida, an apartment building manager was interviewed by the Bureau of Investigation. He said he thought the men and their girlfriends were "gangsters" with their new cars, fancy clothes, and cash. For his own safety the man asked no questions and did not report the group to the authorities.

Always alert to potential danger, the planned three- or four-month stay was cut short. Van Meter returned to Chicago, while Pierpont, Makley, Clark, and two of the women made a 3,000-mile trip to Arizona in January 1934. For some reason, Dillinger and Hamilton stayed in Florida. The *Chicago Tribune* wrote a tongue-in-cheek article reporting Dillinger being spotted from Canada to Mexico and all points in between, even buying houses in Indiana and fishing poles in New York City. Dillinger wrote to his niece, Mary, on New Year's Day, "They blame me for most everything nowadays, but it doesn't make any difference."

Dillinger has probably been the focus of more attention than any other man in the history of crime. Yet discovering where he was or exactly what happened on specific days is difficult. In addition, differences of opinion as to what people witnessed vary widely. As might be suspected, relatives, associates, and Dillinger himself would tell one story, while others testified to a different set of facts. No doubt the most controversial episode in Dillinger's life, other than his death, involved the robbery of the First National Bank of East Chicago, Indiana, on January 15, 1934. The reason for the dispute is that for the first time the charge was made that a man—a police officer no less—had been killed by Dillinger himself. It has been called the "point of no return" for the Hoosier bandit. He later claimed his innocence to his family about the shooting, but allegedly admitted to the shooting to his lawyer. Even decades after the incident, Dillinger family members have threatened lawsuits over the use of the term "killer" rather than "outlaw" when their famous relative was written about.

Weaving together the various stories about the East Chicago bank job, it appears that sometime between New Year's Day 1934 and January 14 Dillinger was reported to have returned to the Chicago area from Florida with Hamilton. Dillinger had supposedly been sighted in both Chicago and Florida, adding to the confusion. It seems clear that Dillinger pulled the East Chicago job without the knowledge of most of his gang. He robbed the bank with little or no planning, something he rarely did. Hitting a bank in East Chicago, where Dillinger allegedly had police connections, was not surprising. This particular robbery may also have been a prearranged operation. The reason for the job was simply that after two months without hitting a bank, Dillinger needed the money.

The evidence seems to indicate that Dillinger arrived with Hamilton in East Chicago around 3:00 p.m. on Monday, January 15. Deposits from the day's business meant this was the time the bank was holding the most money. A third man, who was never identified, served as the getaway driver and stayed with the car. Dillinger, carrying his Thompson submachine gun in what appeared to be a trombone case, called out his customary opening line in a robbery, "This is a stickup. Put your hands up." The other trademarks of Dillinger robberies were the time of the robbery (late afternoon) and his separating the women and children from the men in case there was gunfire. The other Dillinger-like behavior was allowing a customer who had left his money on a counter to keep it. "You go ahead and take your money. We don't want your money. Just the bank's," he said. This was a quip he used often and it endeared him to the public.

As the robbery began, an employee set off the alarm to the police station. The police, once again, thought it a false alarm. When an officer did arrive on the scene he was swiftly disarmed by Dillinger. Other officers, on the verge of entering the bank, backed away and decided to wait for the robbers to come out. The bank's vice president later recounted that Dillinger informed his partner that the police were outside and that they would have to "kill those coppers and get away." Dillinger may have said this, but it sounds more like tough talk from a gangster movie. Ever the jokester, Dillinger pointed to his submachine gun and said, "Oh, don't be afraid of this. I'm not sure it will even shoot." This line rings closer to the truth than the threat to kill "coppers." With twenty to thirty customers and employees inside the bank, Dillinger had his hands full covering the group. The Thompson, with its attached fifty-round drum of bullets, had captured the attention of most. A nervous Hamilton was emptying the cash from behind the tellers' cages. Again, as was usual for Dillinger, he directed Hamilton to take his time. "Don't hurry. Get all that dough," he said.

The take for this mid-January job was $20,000. Using a disarmed policeman and a bank employee as human shields, Dillinger and Hamilton walked out the bank's front door into the street. As he left Dillinger said to the hostage, "You go first. They might as well shoot you as me." While there was a crowd outside, it was quiet. Also waiting were seven policemen, armed and hiding behind cars and in storefronts. The two hostages and two robbers were almost to the open door of the getaway car when policeman William Patrick O'Malley yelled something at the hostage next to Dillinger. The hostage turned, giving O'Malley a clear shot. The officer fired, hitting Dillinger a reported four times in the chest; the rounds were deflected by the bulletproof vest he wore. In response, Dillinger pushed the hostage aside, shouted a curse, and let loose with a burst from his Thompson toward O'Malley. He was heard to have uttered to O'Malley as he fired, "You asked for it." A fellow officer, Hobart Wilgus, testified that Dillinger and O'Malley shot at the same time. Wilgus reported that O'Malley had been struck by eight bullets, all of which went through him. O'Malley, who was forty-three years old and the married father of three, was dead by the time he hit the pavement.

Hamilton then decided to chase one of the policemen who was running down the street. Having left the cover of his hostage, Hamilton was fired on, taking an estimated seven bullets. Dillinger, never one to leave a pal behind, managed under heavy gunfire to get Hamilton and the money into the front seat of the getaway car. The driver dropped the car into gear, hit the accelerator, and they were off.

Dillinger, the wisecracking gentleman bank robber with the crooked smile, had now allegedly killed a policeman. He always

denied he had killed O'Malley or that he was even in East Chicago
that day. In a way the legend that Dillinger was a poor guy
robbing rich banks also died that day. Many in the public now
saw the Mooresville native in a much different light. The robbery
was covered by the *New York Times*, which led with the headline
"Outlaws Rob Bank, Kill Policeman: Band Believed to be Dillinger
Gang Shoots Way Through 8 Officers in East Chicago."

The three men sped off in a blue getaway car with police firing
at them. Dillinger nemesis Leach sent out his state police to pursue
the trio, although he was not sure where the gang was heading.
The car was found the next day, January 16, in Chicago. It had
bullet holes on the outside and blood on the seat cushions inside.
The stains were from Hamilton, who had been severely wounded.
A shady physician in Chicago attended to the wounded crook and
then charged Dillinger $5,000. Dillinger also had to pay $100 a day
for a week to care for Hamilton until his family from Indiana could
pick him up.

The rest of Dillinger's gang was far from Chicago. Makley,
Pierpont, Clark and their molls left Florida in early January,
arriving a week later in Tucson, Arizona. The other member of the
gang, Van Meter, had decided not to make the trip west. Warm
weather and the assumption of safety a thousand miles from the
Midwest were the major reasons Tucson was chosen. The sleepy
western town may have seemed an odd choice for a hideout, but it
was also close to Mexico, a place where Dillinger had on more than
one occasion said he might wish to "retire" and "quit the game."

Meanwhile, Dillinger visited his father on January 17, claiming
that he had just returned from Florida. Freely traveling the state
of Indiana as a hunted man said much about the ineffectiveness of

those pursuing him. Dillinger then returned to Chicago, picked up Frechette, and saw an attorney to move her divorce proceedings along so they could be married. They bought a new car in Saint Louis, his usual auto of choice—a Hudson Terraplane. The salesman, clearly not knowing who he was dealing with, jabbed Dillinger in the ribs and asked if he trusted his "wife" to take it for a test drive. When the man did so, his elbow hit the shoulder holster inside his customer's coat. Dillinger laughed, paid the dealer cash for the car, and the couple left, heading west for Arizona on Route 66. The only excitement on the trip was a traffic ticket Dillinger received in Albuquerque, New Mexico.

After the East Chicago bank job, Dillinger was a changed man. While denying he had killed anyone, the episode in East Chicago seemed to weigh on him. He started taking fewer chances and became more serious about life. Once he said a man had a right to defend himself, seeming to justify what happened in East Chicago. While Dillinger may have been more somber, his partners were not. They had gotten caught up in the relaxed atmosphere of the Southwest and began to make mistakes. What happened next was a mix of bad luck and blunders on the part of the gang and some good work by the Tucson police department.

Feeling safe, Clark and Makley started drinking and talking too much. The hotel where the two men were staying caught fire early in the morning of Tuesday, January 22. When Clark and Makley discovered that their money and guns were still in their room, they tipped the firemen to retrieve their luggage. Wondering what was so heavy in the suitcases (they were filled with machine guns and ammunition), the firemen were even more puzzled when they were given $50 for their efforts. The next day the men identified Clark and Makley in a detective magazine they happened to be reading. The crooks also brought attention to themselves by their expensive clothing and new automobiles. By January 25 the police had begun following Makley, and picked him up without a fight in a store where he was buying a police radio. He was unarmed and did not put up a struggle. Denying that he was Makley, he was taken to the police station and booked anyway.

The capture of Clark was not quite so easy. The police, following Clark, were unaware of Makley's capture. Clark had rented a small house, and it was there the police decided to apprehend him. One plainclothes policeman went to the door in a Western Union Telegram delivery hat with a letter for a "Mr. Long." Clark's girlfriend opened the door and said she would take it. "No, personal delivery mail," was the answer. Clark came out of the back bedroom and went to the door. When the policeman pulled his gun a fistfight began and the two men, joined by a second policeman, wrestled their way to the back of the house. Clark was finally hit on the head with the butt of a gun. The stash of weapons found on the premises was large. Public Enemy Number Two was in custody at the minor expense of a policeman's broken finger. Clark's girlfriend had slammed the door on his hand.

Next came Pierpont. Handsome Harry, unaware the gang was being picked off one by one, was also being watched. (He had foolishly chatted with two policemen the week before, pretending to be a tourist from Florida.) Kinder, Pierpont's moll, arrived at the Clark house but quickly left upon seeing blood and the disorder inside the home. A neighbor remembered the license plate number as Pierpoint and Kinder headed out of town. The Tucson police stopped Pierpont for a minor traffic violation, no tourist sticker on his windshield. When asked how to get one, the police told Pierpont they would help him. Without asking, one of the police got into the backseat of Pierpont's car for the ride to headquarters. The two men eyed each other in the rearview mirror during the drive. The policeman had placed a gun from his pocket in his lap.

Arriving at the police station, Pierpont and Kinder calmly went inside thinking they could bluff their way out of this unforeseen interruption in their escape. But when Pierpont saw Clark's luggage he realized that this was more than an issue of a missing tourist sticker. Pierpont reached for one of three guns he was carrying, but the lawmen were too quick for him. He was grabbed, disarmed, and handcuffed all in one swift act. (One of the guns turned out to be the weapon that had killed Sheriff Sarber in Lima, Ohio.) Although he, too, denied who he was, fingerprints confirmed that the Tucson police had captured Handsome Harry Pierpont. Complimenting the police, Pierpont later said, "These cops out here ain't like the kind they have in Indiana. They pull too fast for us."

How the gang communicated with one another has always been a mystery. They did seem to know that the house where Clark was captured would be the meeting place for the group. Dillinger and Frechette did not know as they drove into Tucson that their friends had all been captured. As they pulled up to Clark's dark house in the new Terraplane, two police officers were waiting inside and a third was watching from the street. Leaving Frechette in the car with her new puppy, Dillinger walked up to the house and, as had Pierpont's girlfriend, noticed that there had been a scuffle. He quickly turned back toward the car only to be faced by the outside policeman who asked him, "What do you want?" Dillinger replied in a cool manner, "I am at the wrong house." The other two officers emerged from inside and countered just as steadily, "Oh no you're not."

"What's this all about?" Dillinger asked, as if puzzled. At first he claimed he was a salesman from Wisconsin. But Dillinger's true identity was soon learned. Being told to raise his hands and failing to do so, one of the Tucson policemen drew his gun on Dillinger. "Reach for the moon or I'll cut you in two," he yelled. Dillinger at first slowly raised his hands, then made a move for his gun. The Old West lawmen were too quick though. They shoved him, grabbed his coat, and pointed two guns in his face. "My God, how did you know I was in town?" asked Dillinger. "I'll be the laughingstock of the courts. How did I know a hick town police force would ever suspect me?" Frechette and her puppy were also under arrest.

It was all over. In less than eight hours the Tucson police department had accomplished what law enforcement agencies, bank security, private detectives, and even the Dillinger-obsessed Leach and his Indiana State Police had been unable to do—capture the Dillinger Gang. More important was what the Tucson lawmen found on Dillinger. He had been carrying one gun and was wearing a money belt with at least $2,000 in it. Several of the five-dollar bills were traced by the Bureau back to the East Chicago robbery. A critical connection had been made.

The gang was transferred from the Tucson city jail to the county jail. Dillinger, who usually remained quite calm, repeatedly yelled threats at his captors and vowed to break out of jail. When he calmed down he said, "Here, you guys were smart getting us one at a time." The newspapers across the country made much of the frontier setting where the capture of the gang took place. They wrote of "quick draws," mentioned famous cowboys from the movies, and printed photos of the police in their Stetson hats. The story even made it into the *New York Times*.

On Saturday, January 26, Dillinger, Makley, Clark, Pierpont, and the three women appeared in the Pima County Courthouse for a preliminary hearing. The room was full of reporters who had flown in from all over the country, even large cities back East. The court learned little during the hearing, with Dillinger even denying he was Dillinger. "I ain't Dillinger," he said. Pierpont responded disrespectfully to the judge with wisecracks. But the guns and money, almost $50,000 in cash and jewels among the four men, earned each of them a $100,000 bail for being fugitives from justice. Bail for the women was set at $5,000.

On his way out of the courtroom, Dillinger leaned over, smiled, and kissed Frechette. Taken by the romantic scene, one reporter in the courtroom wrote, "Dillinger has none of the looks of the conventional killer. Given a little more time and a wider circle of acquaintances, one can see that he might presently become the central figure in a nationwide campaign, largely female, to prevent his frying in the electric chair." At this time, the term "killer" could be used with suspects without the adjective "alleged." The gun found on Pierpont from the Sarber killing and the money on Dillinger from the East Chicago bank job placed both men in serious legal jeopardy.

Loosening up in his jail cell, Dillinger said, "I'm an expert in my business. I can play tag with the police anytime. They . . . don't know what's going on. The dumbest ones in the world are the Chicago kind." He added that there was no evidence he had robbed any banks or killed anyone. In custody, Dillinger usually made wisecracks and played up to his captors to appear harmless. Dillinger even told gawkers who filed through the county jail to see him, "Vote for the sheriff in the next election," suggesting he grudgingly admired being outsmarted this time. From his quotes in the newspapers, Dillinger was more meek than menacing. He talked about "beating the rap" and said his only bad habit, since he smoked and drank little, was robbing banks. He confessed to helping his former fellow inmates escape from Michigan City. And when he heard his father was glad he had been captured without bloodshed, Dillinger called his dad a "good scout" and said he wished he "had taken up some other line of business."

The gang hired a Tucson lawyer. Three states—Indiana, Ohio,

Tucson, Arizona, police watch over a sullen Harry Pierpont after his capture in 1934.

A still dapper Dillinger awaits his fate after his and other members of his gang's arrest in Tucson.

and Wisconsin—sent teams of attorneys and lawmen to obtain the suspects' extradition. Indiana wanted Dillinger for the purported East Chicago robbery and shooting of O'Malley. Ohio authorities sought Pierpont, Makley, and Clark for allegedly killing Sarber. The day after his capture, a grand jury in Lake Chicago, Indiana, agreed that there was enough evidence to indict Dillinger on the charge of murdering O'Malley. Several eyewitnesses testified to the grand jury about the shooting. Realizing that the charges against him had the possibility of the death penalty, Dillinger wanted to go to Wisconsin. Capital punishment was not practiced there and the charge was only the Racine bank robbery, not murder.

Finally catching up with, if not actually catching his man, Leach arrived in Tucson and went directly to the county jail. Still angry with Leach about jailing his mother to get information, Pierpont threatened to kill the state policeman. He had actually followed Leach one day in downtown Indianapolis and it was all Dillinger could do to stop Pierpont from shooting the lawman in the back. Leach, taunting Pierpont, said, "There's a man who really loves his mother." Pierpont went berserk yelling, "I should have killed you when I had the chance. When I get out of here the first thing I am going to do is kill you, you rat!" Pierpont's behavior became more erratic in the Tucson jail. He ranted that no jail could hold him and threatened to return and "kill you all" when he got out.

Moving down the cell row Leach went to the man he had traveled two days to see. Stopping at Dillinger's cell he said, "Well, we meet again, John." They had first met in Ohio after the Dayton capture. Author John Toland in his book *The Dillinger Days* has written that the pursuer and his quarry were "obsessed" with each other. With reluctance Dillinger shook hands with him through the bars. Leach asked Dillinger if he was ready to go back to Indiana with him. "I'm in no hurry," Dillinger replied. "I haven't a thing to do when I get there."

The issue of whether Dillinger was in East Chicago and had pulled the robbery where O'Malley had been killed was to be a critical one. Was it Dillinger who fired the fatal shots or was he even at the scene of the robbery? Dillinger had convinced his family that he was not there. Kinder insisted even after Dillinger's death that he was not in East Chicago. Audrey Hancock, Dillinger's sister, also maintained to the Bureau and other authorities that her brother had not killed O'Malley or anyone else. But he was carrying East Chicago bank money in Arizona, and a policeman who had witnessed the killing arrived in Tucson and identified Dillinger as the shooter.

The Pima County sheriff in Tucson, while beefing up security at the jail, allowed two thousand visitors to file past the four men in their cells. Even the governor of Arizona called on Dillinger. Reporters were allowed to interview the gang. They all maintained their innocence, saying they had been nowhere near any of the crimes, especially the Sarber and O'Malley shootings. Dillinger again expressed regret over the distress he had caused his father back in Mooresville. He added, referring to himself, "Well, that's how life goes. We can't all be angels." Giving an Indianapolis newspaper reporter his lucky rabbit's foot Dillinger quipped, "You may as well have this. I am running out of luck anyway."

Extradition proceedings began in earnest with Indiana governor Paul V. McNutt indicating his willingness to work with Ohio's governor. Robert Estill, prosecuting attorney for East Chicago, arrived as Indiana wanted Dillinger, while Ohio officials sought his three henchmen. Dillinger talked openly about the Racine robbery with Wisconsin officials. He said he was glad there was no shooting and basically admitted that he had done the job. Joking with the Wisconsin representatives, Dillinger said, "I want to go back with you fellows. You look more sociable." A local Arizona newspaper observed the four prisoners to be above average in intelligence, well spoken, and if not in custody able to pass for "honorable and respectable citizens." All four men gladly signed extradition papers to return to Wisconsin. But then, making deals on the side, the Tucson prosecutor changed his mind and let Leach from Indiana have Dillinger and allowed the other three men to be taken to Ohio.

Upon hearing he was heading back to Indiana, not Wisconsin, the usually composed Dillinger violently protested. "Where's my mouthpiece [lawyer]?" he yelled, "You're shanghaiing me! They can't take me without a hearing." Strongly resisting his removal, it took five men to get Dillinger out of his cell. In spite of his objections and resistance, he was placed on a chartered airplane on Monday, January 29, for the trip to Indiana. Wisconsin officials came up empty-handed with nothing more than a machine gun autographed by Dillinger to take back home. One angry Wisconsin representative noted that Indiana officials had either paroled or let each gang member escape at one time or another. He voiced the hope that "the negligence of the officers of that state will never be repeated."

The flight back to Indiana with Public Enemy Number One made eight stops. Changing planes several times, Dillinger and the Crown Point, Indiana, officials flew from Tucson to Douglas, Arizona, and from there through El Paso, Abilene, Fort Worth, and Dallas, Texas. It was then on to Little Rock, Arkansas, and Memphis, Tennessee.

The final Saint Louis to Chicago leg of the flight was made in a Ford trimotor airplane. The plane arrived in Chicago at 6:00 p.m. the next day, January 30, twenty-four hours after leaving Arizona. A photographer for a Chicago newspaper purchased the four empty seats on the flight, making sure no other journalist could have access to Dillinger. The report that Dillinger confessed to killing O'Malley while on the long plane trip is doubtful.

There are two descriptions of Dillinger's flight back to his home state from Saint Louis. A stewardess later recalled that she felt sorry for the prisoner "who looked like a little puppy with his tail between his legs." She gave him a pillow, chewing gum, a blanket, an aspirin, and a glass of water. The other witness, the photographer, rendered a different image of the bandit. Allowed to take a few pictures of the prisoner handcuffed to his seat, the man said after the brief flight, "I met plenty of tough guys, but I don't think I ever met a tougher one than Dillinger." The photographer's estimation of the outlaw would prove to be more accurate than the one of the stewardess. Dillinger soon proved to be no "puppy."

6

The Great Escape

The events of early March 1934 guaranteed lasting fame for John Dillinger. There were rumors of an escape on his return to Indiana from Arizona. After all, his partners Homer Van Meter and John Hamilton were still at large. To assure that there were no rescue attempts, extraordinary security measures were set into place. More than thirty Chicago policemen wearing bulletproof vests and lugging an array of armaments from machine guns to pistols were on hand when Dillinger's plane arrived at Midway Airport a little after 6:00 p.m. on January 30. Serving as backup to the local police presence were thirty troopers from the Indiana State Police. An additional sixty local officers were on duty just to maintain order at the airport.

Dillinger's arrival on that snowy Chicago night has been well documented on film and in photographs. Indiana's own celebrity outlaw was now living up to his reputation. Lights and flashes from the cameras made the night seem like day as the press shouted questions. Amid the impressive show of force was Dillinger, handcuffed to a county deputy sheriff. He was hustled to a waiting police car, part of a thirteen-vehicle caravan. The drive from the airport to Crown Point, Indiana, the county seat of Lake County where the East Chicago police shooting had occurred, was thirty miles.

The considerable display of manpower by law enforcement was

not merely for show. A high-ranking Chicago lawman had given
the order, "If any effort is made to raid the caravan and release
Dillinger, or if he makes a break to escape, kill him at once!" The fact
that there was press in the group heading for the Lake County Jail
may also have assured his safety. Upon its arrival in Indiana, the
parade of police cars was described by the Crown Point newspaper:
"John Dillinger came to town Tuesday evening. He was met by
a volunteer reception committee of some four or five hundred
citizens gathered from all parts to catch a glimpse of the noted
bank robber and killer." The term "killer" was again used by the
press at this time, suggesting the guilt of the suspect, with no fear
of legal repercussion.

The two major players in Lake County who would be dealing
with Dillinger's case were Sheriff Lillian Holley and the county
prosecutor, Robert Estill. Indiana's only female sheriff, Holley
inherited the job when her husband had been killed the year before
in a shoot-out. It was no small task the forty-year-old woman had
taken on at the request of the county commissioner. Lake County
was second in state population only to Marion County, where
the state capital Indianapolis was located. One of Holley's duties
was overseeing the Lake County jail in Crown Point, now home
to Dillinger. A mix of feminine and masculine, Holley belonged to
ladies' clubs and missionary societies and yet carried a pistol.

Estill was a bespectacled man in his fifties with thinning hair
parted in the middle. He looked like a lawyer. Estill had made the
journey to Arizona to lobby for Dillinger's return to his jurisdiction.
There was speculation that the prosecutor had hopes for higher
political office—maybe even governor. This ambition may have
clouded his decision that night when he made a serious error of

judgment. Estill allowed a press conference with his prisoner to take place. Dillinger, apparently recovered from his cross-country trip, his first on an airplane, was no longer the "puppy dog" he had seemed during the flight. He immediately turned his considerable charm toward the press. Not thinking amid the excitement, Estill failed to grasp the harm it caused allowing Dillinger access to the media.

Thirty reporters squeezed into a room in the Lake County Jail. Outside there were an estimated five hundred onlookers. Immediately the questions began. "Are you glad to see Indiana again?" asked one newspaperman. "About as glad as Indiana is to see me," Dillinger swiftly responded. This first press conference

The famous photograph of Dillinger with his arm on the shoulder of Lake County prosecutor Robert Estill at the Lake County Jail. At the far left is Sheriff Lillian Holley. Notice how the fingers of Dillinger's right hand are formed in the shape of a gun.

probably set the tone for what became the "Dillinger as Celebrity" legend. He was chewing gum, smiling his crooked smile, enjoying himself. This was the first look the public had gotten of Dillinger and both press and the prisoner were enjoying themselves.

Estill, in a decision that he regretted for the rest of his life, posed with his prisoner. Some have suggested the next few minutes torpedoed any political ambitions the Lake County prosecutor harbored. A Chicago photographer asked Estill to put his arm around Dillinger. Amazingly he did. Then Dillinger put his arm on Estill's shoulder. A better "buddy" picture could not have been created. One of the photographs has Dillinger with his hand in the shape of a gun—three fingers bent, index finger pointing down, and the thumb looking like the hammer of a pistol. Some thought this was a signal to friends on the outside to slip a gun into the jail. But the press conference occurred so quickly that this is doubtful. Sheriff Holley also appears in the photograph, standing next to Estill.

The public loved the Dillinger/Estill pose. But more serious lawmen immediately saw the photograph as a public relations nightmare. The president of the Chicago Crime Commission said, "I was shocked at seeing newspaper photographs of a prosecutor who is about to prosecute a vicious murderer posing with his arm around a murderer's neck, both of them smiling and exhibiting friendship." He added, "Perhaps it isn't unethical, but it is certain that such familiarity breeds contempt for law enforcement in the minds of criminals." The image of the two men was to become a mainstay in the gallery of Dillinger photographs.

The captured bank robber (he had confessed to the Racine job in hopes of being sent to Wisconsin) continued to take questions from the press. When asked where his hat was, Dillinger said they had stolen it in Tucson, along with his money. Playing both victim and nice guy, he spun his tale of a bum rap that led him to a life of crime. He maintained he was no threat to the public. "I was just an unfortunate boy back in Mooresville," he said. As for helping his ten buddies break out of the Michigan City prison he said, "I met a lot of good fellows. I wanted to help them out. Why not? I stick to my friends, and they stick to me." The next question was, "How long does it take you to go through a bank?" Dillinger replied, tongue in cheek, "One minute and forty seconds flat." Although he never wasted time inside a bank this was, of course, an exaggeration.

Oddly, Estill and Holley allowed the interview to continue. Stranger still, Dillinger kept talking and was getting better at it by the minute. Speaking in generalities, he told of life in Chicago. This included the getaways, shootouts, and his driving ability. He added how the gang moved from neighborhood to neighborhood and house to house, but gave no details. "Those were exciting times," he mused. Dillinger did blame Charles Makley and Russell Clark for their arrest in Arizona. They had tipped the firemen too much to retrieve their suitcases. "If the saps had made it only a couple of bucks, we'd still be safe and happy," he said.

It seemed at times as though the interview would never end. The topics ranged from cartoons to the U.S. president. Dillinger noted that "The Three Little Pigs" was one of his favorite cartoons and the nation's number one bank robber endorsed Franklin D. Roosevelt and his Bank Recovery Act. Asked if it was him who had mailed Matt Leach the book *How to Be a Detective*, he replied, "Well I was there when it was sent." Commenting on his personal habits, Dillinger revealed that he drank and smoked very little. "I guess my only bad habit is robbing banks," repeating a line he had used in Arizona.

One topic Dillinger became extremely defensive about, though, was the alleged killing of Sergeant William O'Malley in East Chicago. Knowing that this was the most dangerous charge he faced, he flatly denied it. "I never killed O'Malley. They can't hold me for that. When that job was pulled I was in Florida. I never had anything to do with that East Chicago stickup," Dillinger said. In part to explain the East Chicago money found on him and to protect the wounded John Hamilton, Dillinger added that the money had come from the "dead" Hamilton. Dillinger was to deliver the money, seven thousand dollars from the robbery, to Hamilton's children. Hoping to convince lawmen that Hamilton had been killed, Dillinger sadly concluded: "Poor old John. Well, he's dead." A very much alive Hamilton, along with Homer Van Meter, were actually in Chicago attempting to join forces with Baby Face Nelson.

As the evening finally drew to a close, Dillinger ended the exchange with the press by saying, "Now you see fellas, I ain't such a bad guy at heart. I try to be right." For good measure he added, "I like Mr. Estill. And Mrs. Holley [the sheriff] seems like a fine lady." With that line he was led away to his cell.

Dillinger clearly charmed the press and thoroughly enjoyed himself. Stories in the next day's papers referred to him as "suave," "articulate," and even "swashbuckling." He was relaxed, humorous, well-spoken, and even sympathetic—not the ruthless killer many had been expecting. One paper said the half-hour interview was done "with an air that demonstrated Dillinger to be as mild-mannered a man as ever shot up a bank." Even the *New York Times* gave Dillinger's remarkable act good reviews. Bryan Burrough, author of *Public Enemies: America's Greatest Crime Wave and the Birth of the FBI, 1933-34*, concluded it was "the performance of a lifetime."

The Crown Point news conference, according to author William Beverly, allowed Dillinger, for the first time, to come across as a human being. He could be photographed and quoted. He could tell his story of being a small-time kid who fell under the influence of hardened criminals in prison, then made it big robbing banks and living a life of luxury. Dillinger threw off one-liners and seemed no threat to the public at all. Within twenty-four hours Dillinger had turned from a screaming, seemingly terrified crook into a polished, charming celebrity in the making. A Chicago newspaperman wrote, "His diction was perfectly amazing . . . his poise no less so . . . he rates in the eyes of observers as the most amazing specimen of his kind ever seen outside a moving picture."

Meanwhile, as Dillinger had been winging his way across the country, the status of his three accused associates and two women back in Arizona was being resolved. Billie Frechette, with the authorities unable to connect her to the gang due to an alias she used, was able to walk out of jail with her puppy, a free woman. Mary Kinder was a different story. Her involvement with Harry Pierpont, and the fact she had two brothers in prison, made her a person of interest to lawmen.

On January 29 the four prisoners—Pierpont, Clark, Makley, and Kinder—were placed on a train with Leach. Fifteen hundred Tucson citizens were on hand as the train left the station. The prisoners reached Chicago two days later. Kinder and Pierpont had asked to be married in the Tucson jail, but the request was denied. During the two days on the rails, Leach and Pierpont reached a truce. Leach even allowed Kinder to sit next to her boyfriend. Pierpont held his own press conference on the train, linking his bank jobs to the familiar Robin Hood metaphor—stealing from the rich who had stolen from the poor.

While Pierpont and Leach may have made up, the Indiana State Police captain had left behind no friends in Tucson. The small-town police were expecting a significant sum of money for their success in capturing the Dillinger Gang. Leach stiffed them. When he offered the Arizona lawmen only three hundred dollars, they erupted. One of the policemen seized Leach by the collar and called him a "double crossing rat." Leach had gladly boarded the train with his prisoners and headed east. Once in Chicago it was a direct trip to the penitentiary at Michigan City for his guests. Again, the police presence was overwhelming. One estimate had 150 lawmen accompanying the three men back to prison. Makley for one had no wish to return. He was alleged to have said, "Do me a favor. Shoot

IHS, JAY SMALL POSTCARD COLLECTION, P. 391

The exterior of the Lake County Jail in Crown Point, Indiana.

me through the head so I won't have to go back in there." The three men were eventually shipped to Ohio for Sherriff Jess Sarber's murder and Kinder was later released.

With Pierpont, Makley, and Clark safely behind the bars again, attention turned to making sure Dillinger did not escape. There were rumors that a breakout plan was in the works. Inside the jail, an around-the-clock watch of the prisoner was under way with a policeman keeping a machine gun pointed at Dillinger. There were six steel doors between the prisoner and the outside. An armed Holley sat up most of each night as an added precaution. Guards stood watch outside the jail in addition to a number of armed volunteers. The Indiana National Guard was also on duty with their Browning Automatic Rifles, able to spew 120 bullets per minute and pierce bulletproof vests.

The day after his arrival, January 31, Dillinger hired Chicago attorney Louis Piquett (pronounced "picket"). The two men had never met, but knew each other by reputation. A well-known criminal lawyer, Piquett was capable of playing both sides of the legal fence in defending his clients. He would use the laws to protect a defendant's rights while at the same time employing tactics that bordered on the unethical. Although he never graduated from law school, Piquett was effective in the courtroom, as he was both eloquent and flamboyant. The two men met and decided that the defense Piquett used would be simple. In spite of several witnesses identifying Dillinger as the shooter, Piquett maintained that his client was not present in East Chicago. In fact, he was in Florida when O'Malley was killed. In private with his lawyer, Dillinger was quite nervous, knowing if this defense failed it would mean death in the electric chair.

A Crown Point deputy sheriff, who got to know Dillinger during his stay in jail, became convinced his prisoner was not a killer. "He was tough, but not the tough 'killer' type," the deputy later said. "He would have killed if his life had been at stake, but as far as being a deliberate killer, I can't believe John Dillinger was that way. I'm skeptical as to whether they ever would have found him guilty of that East Chicago charge. I asked him about it a couple of times and he said, 'I wasn't there, but I got some of the money.' I don't believe the man was there." Another deputy thought Dillinger only dangerous if threatened. "He'd give up if cornered, and you'd better give up if he had you cornered," he observed.

Dillinger's father visited his son in Crown Point on February 1. John Sr. had hired an attorney from Indianapolis, but his son declined, preferring to go with big-city lawyer Piquett. Dillinger was not comfortable with the visit, feeling guilty over what he had put his father through. He even apologized before borrowing ten dollars. Still blaming himself, John Sr. returned to the episode of ten years earlier. He believed the lack of fifteen dollars to secure a good attorney and his own bad advice for his son to plead guilty had led him down this road of crime.

At the arraignment on February 8, Dillinger was handcuffed to a deputy sheriff clad in a bulletproof vest. Although flash bulbs went off when Dillinger entered the courtroom, the prisoner had lost the flair he had displayed the week before. His attorney had lost none of his. To put the prosecutor on the defensive Piquett made much of the heavy guard around Dillinger. "Why don't you call back your men with their machine guns?" Piquett asked. "Why don't you stand Dillinger against a wall and shoot him down. There's no need to throw away the state's money on this kind of mockery. Your

honor, even Christ had a fairer trial than this." Dillinger loved it.
"Atta boy, counsel," he whispered to Piquett.

Five men had already testified Dillinger had killed O'Malley in
East Chicago. The prosecutor had five more witnesses ready to take
the stand to repeat the same story. Piquett and Estill next wrangled
over trial dates. Piquett wanted four months to prepare, while Estill
asked Judge William J. Murray to go to trial in ten days. Murray
gave the defense a month to get ready. Estill was accused of being
too kindhearted toward his prisoner, but the prosecutor responded
that asking for the death penalty did not mean the process could
not be done in a humane way. Although Estill suggested he had
turned down a guilty plea from the defense in return for a sentence
of life in prison rather than the electric chair, Piquett denied such
an offer had been made.

*A handcuffed Dillinger at his arraignment in Lake County. To Dillinger's left is
attorney Joseph Ryan, whom he dropped in favor of Louis Piquett.*

On February 12 the bickering between the attorneys resumed. A request to return Dillinger to Arizona by Piquett was quashed. Next, Estill asked Murray to move Dillinger from Crown Point to Michigan City. For all of the apparent goodwill toward his prisoner, Estill was concerned about an escape attempt. Holley bristled at suggestions of moving Dillinger to Michigan City because her jail could not hold her high-profile prisoner. Piquett quickly replied, "That's what I thought. But, of course, I don't want to embarrass Mrs. Holley. I appreciate that she's a woman and if she is afraid of escape." Furious, Holley interrupted, "I'm not afraid of an escape. I can take care of John Dillinger or any other prisoner." Murray, in either a move to defend the competency of his facility and jail personnel or Holley's integrity, refused to allow the transfer. "A hundred men couldn't take him out of the jail," said Murray.

Piquett was still putting together a defense that Dillinger was in Florida. He even toyed with the idea of hiring a professional racecar driver to prove a trip from Florida to northern Indiana in twenty-three hours was impossible. As his lawyer worked, Dillinger spent time playing cards, reading magazines, and writing letters. While allowed no newspapers, some said he had a Bible. Billie Frechette arrived in mid-February for a visit. While Piquett was allowed to see Dillinger in private, Frechette was not.

Frechette told Holley that she was "Mrs. Dillinger." Holley had no apparent experience with Native Americans and thought Frechette might possibly be part Mexican or Italian due to her "swarthy" skin color (swarthy was the term used at this time for any nonblack person with dark skin.) Holley guessed Frechette to be about 140 pounds, five feet five or five feet six inches tall, with very dark eyes and a "full round face." Holley had Frechette undress and personally searched her before she was allowed to see Dillinger, whom she viewed through a wire-mesh screen. After the visit, Dillinger asked his lawyer to deliver a "love note" to Frechette. Upon reading it, Piquett was shocked. It contained a plan to dynamite the jail followed by a machine-gun battle with the guards. Nothing, of course, came of this ill-conceived plan.

Dillinger had concocted a more realistic plan to get out of the Crown Point jail—one that brought him additional fame and added to the legend being built around him. The escape and how it was carried out has also been the subject of much controversy. The debate is over whether or not Dillinger broke out of the jail on his own or had aid from either the inside or outside. Dillinger appeared confident the defense his lawyer was building would succeed. But then on Saturday morning, March 3, 1934, he decided to take matters into his own hands.

The plan was centered on the use of a gun that may or may not have been real. If it was indeed a real pistol, then it would have been smuggled in from the outside. How this may have been done has never been fully explained. Access to Dillinger was limited to his attorney and a carefully searched Frechette. The second source for the gun, or what looked like a gun, would have been one that Dillinger produced himself. That gun, according to Dillinger, was made by wood from a washboard, stained black with shoe polish, and imbedded with metal from old razor blades to give the weapon a realistic look. The fake gun had no handle and was therefore difficult to grip.

The weapon became the stuff of both folklore and debate. Did Dillinger really whittle it? Was it made of wood or soap? Was it a real gun smuggled in by his lawyer or someone who worked inside the jail? One piece of evidence that points to the gun being fake was that his fellow prisoners in Crown Point nicknamed Dillinger "John the Whittler." A third option for the appearance of the gun in Dillinger's possession would be that the weapon was fake, but had been crafted by an expert on the outside and then smuggled into the jail. A final story suggested there were two guns—both a real and a fake—to cover for the real one being smuggled in.

Whether the gun was real or not made little difference as far as what happened next. After a month in custody, those guarding Dillinger in the Crown Point jail had become lax. The round-the-clock watches had stopped. On the morning of March 3 an elderly jail worker and his two helpers walked into a large exercise room on the jail's second floor. They were there to deliver soap and supplies to the cellblock for Saturday night baths to the fourteen prisoners, including Dillinger. Unfortunately, the worker and his helpers failed to make sure the prisoners were locked up before entering the cellblock. The old man soon found what appeared to be an automatic pistol shoved into his side. Dillinger wasted no time, saying, "Get inside quick or I'll kill you." The elderly worker replied, "What's the matter,

ASSOCIATED PRESS

Herbert Youngblood of Gary, Indiana, was being held on murder charges when he escaped from the Lake County Jail with Dillinger on March 3, 1934.

John, haven't we been good to you?" Dillinger only responded, "Never mind," and told him to call the warden. He refused. Dillinger then asked Herbert Youngblood, an African American in jail on a murder charge, if he wished to join him. In his mind Youngblood believed he had nothing to lose and agreed. Locking the two helpers in a cell, Dillinger, Youngblood, and the elderly man moved down the hallway.

While the jail's floor plan was complex, Dillinger seemed to know his way around the facility. The threesome ran into the fingerprint expert, Ernest Blunk, who became the next man to be faced with what looked like the barrel of a .45 automatic. Blunk, as well as a few others, were later charged with helping Dillinger to escape. One source accused the fingerprint man of furnishing the gun and being the "go-between" who paid bribes to outsiders. With Blunk in tow, the jail worker was no longer needed and he, too, was locked in a cell. He did warn Dillinger that there were at least a dozen guards out front and that he would never make it out of the jail. "Watch me," was Dillinger's only reply. Blunk was then ordered to call the warden, who was also entrapped and placed in a cell.

Traveling through the jail's corridors, Dillinger and Youngblood captured guards two and three at a time. One man was even dozing. All the while, Dillinger, Youngblood, and the reluctant Blunk were moving closer to the outside doors. It was reported, in Blunk's defense, that Dillinger kept the gun in his back. Dillinger made threats to kill anyone who did not cooperate. He also said as they moved through the jail, "Contrary to what people say, I'm no killer. But I'm gonna get out of here." As they continued on there were no glitches. This was possibly due to the fact it was a Saturday morning with few individuals on duty. Another reason there was no opposition or gunfire during the escape was that firearms were not allowed in the cellblock.

One of the guards they ran into, though, was armed with a blackjack (a short, handheld piece of metal wrapped in leather) and began to reach into his pocket for it. "What are you doing here, John?" the guard asked, calling Dillinger by his first name. Nothing if not cool in tight situations, Dillinger saw what was about to happen and cautioned the man, "Don't do it. I don't want to kill you, but I'm getting out of here no matter what happens." This guard thought the gun Dillinger carried was a .38 automatic and had little doubt it was real, a story he stuck to for the rest of his life: "When I hear people say he got out with a wooden gun, I get so mad I could spit. You look down the barrel of (a real) one and you know the difference between a wooden gun and a good one." Blunk agreed, noting, "I didn't know it was a dummy then, but it was the best imitation of a gun I ever saw." Dillinger played up the fact it was a "toy." "See what I locked you monkeys up with?" he bragged. "Nothing but a little piece of wood. Well, so long boys. I'll have to be moving on."

Dillinger, Youngblood, and Blunk moved down from the second to the first floor. They had left five guards, thirteen prisoners, and the warden locked up. The more men he captured the more confident he became. "Be good girls and no one will get hurt," he taunted the two male guards. Two more men were seized, including an Indiana National Guardsman, who Dillinger disarmed. Whether he had a real gun before, he had one now, a .45 automatic. Reaching an office, he picked up more firepower when he found two machine guns lying in the empty room. Dillinger took several dollars from the guards on his way out. Before leaving he was said to have laughed, struck the wooden gun against the metal cell bars, and boastfully said, "This is how tough your jail is. I did it all with my little toy pistol."

Moving next through the jail's kitchen, Dillinger and Youngblood put on hats and raincoats and left the building. Blunk was still with them. The three men had picked up two or three other inmates on their way through the building. On second thought, though, the newest recruits did not relish what they anticipated was waiting for them outside the jail. They decided to return and lock themselves in their cells. In the kitchen Dillinger, Youngblood, and Blunk startled the warden's wife and her mother. The older woman immediately fainted. Her daughter started screaming, "Dillinger's out! Dillinger's out!" When the focus of her fear grabbed her arm she yelled, "My God, it's you!" Both women were placed in a closet. As was his practice with bank robberies, Dillinger was taking his time.

Dillinger, in need of transportation, astoundingly retraced his escape route returning upstairs in search of car keys. When none of those he had locked up had any in their possession, Dillinger asked Blunk for the directions to the nearest garage. With 1930s automobiles unreliable and in frequent need of repair, garages were numerous and there was one close by. Possibly the most amazing, even unbelievable, part of the whole escape was that there were no guards behind the jail, although at least twenty men inside the jail were yelling to those out front. The three men just strolled out the backdoor of the jail and walked one block to the Main Street Garage, entering through its alley entrance.

A garage mechanic, working on a vehicle, was chatting with a postal employee who was killing time before starting his mail route.

Asking for the fastest car in the garage, Dillinger was directed to a black V-8 Ford with a red headlight and siren. Not recognizing him, the two men in the garage thought Dillinger, carrying a machine gun, was a special deputy. They thought that until Dillinger gave the order, "Let's get going." Dillinger took the mechanic, left the mailman behind, and told Blunk to drive. Dillinger joined him in the front seat with Youngblood and the mechanic in the back. What Dillinger did not know was that he was driving Sheriff Holley's car out the front door of the garage.

A Hollywood scriptwriter could not have created this breakout, especially Dillinger quietly driving off in the sheriff's Ford. As they drove out of the garage, Dillinger seemed the only one in the car not surprised he had carried off the escape. Still playing the witty bandit, he quipped, "Maybe I should go back and tell Mrs. Holley I'm leaving. She seemed like an awfully nice lady and I don't want her to feel hurt about all this." The car headed north on Main Street. As they passed a bank, Dillinger considered robbing it, but, not having done his usual homework, passed it by. "Take your time. Take your time," Dillinger told Blunk. "Thirty miles an hour is enough. There's no hurry." When Blunk tried to wreck the car, Dillinger sternly warned he would kill him if he tried a stunt like that again.

Following the routine of bank robbery getaways, the car made turn after turn and kept to back roads. Incredibly relaxed, Dillinger, according to Blunk, began humming and whistling a western song "The Last Roundup" with its refrain, "Get along, little doggies, get along." Dillinger next showed Blunk the fake gun, explaining how he made it. "You wouldn't think a guy could make a break with a peashooter like this would you?" cracked Dillinger. Ever loyal, he also told his fellow passengers he intended to get Pierpont and his other friends out of jail in Ohio. "They'd do as much for me," he said. When they were out of town the mechanic was ordered to take the red light and siren off the front of the sheriff's car.

As the foursome was calmly making their getaway, back in Crown Point it finally dawned on the postal worker in the garage, "That's Dillinger!" He began making phone calls and crying out, "Dillinger's escaped! Dillinger's escaped!" As with many bank robberies, when the alarm had finally been sounded, few believed it was true. "Is that right?" said one disbelieving man. "You're nuts," came the reply from another, "You want us to lock you up?"

One person who did not doubt what had happened was Holley. After a month of closely watching Dillinger, she had decided to sleep in on this particular Saturday morning. When informed of the escape, Holley called it "too ridiculous for words." She later told a newsman that Dillinger took "one chance in a million and all the breaks were with him and against me." Humorist Will Rogers observed, "You can't blame that woman sheriff no more after all because she thought she was depending on men!" Immediately the fact that she was female became an issue. When asked if the job was too big for a woman, she spat back a curse, possibly hoping to sound tough.

In contrast, Dillinger again came out looking like the gentleman bandit. A deputy sheriff who had guarded him said that the outlaw's manner was always respectful and polite, noting, "I never heard him cuss or be abusive in any way, shape or fashion." Regardless of who was cussing, the Crown Point officials were at a loss as to what to do. The fact they sent out the wrong license plate number for the sheriff's car did not help. The "Dillinger Luck" continued to hold.

The getaway, however, did not proceed without incident. The sheriff's car had slid off the road and was stuck in mud twenty-three miles west of Crown Point. Blunk had not done it on purpose; it was an accident. Youngblood and the mechanic attached chains to the tires and in a half hour the group was again on its way. When Dillinger noticed there were no more telephone poles along the highway, therefore no more telephones, he let Blunk and the mechanic out of the car. Giving them eight dollars of the fifteen dollars he had stolen from the jailers, he smiled, shook hands with them, and said, "It's not much, but it's all I can spare. Maybe I can remember you at Christmas." With this last quip, Dillinger and Youngblood were gone.

7

Back in Business—March 1934

John Dillinger's remarkable escape from the Crown Point jail seemed both unbelievable, and yet just something a figure like Dillinger could pull off. In both newspapers and on the radio the news spread—"Dillinger's Out!" and "John Dillinger Escapes." An Arizona newspaper wrote that the escape "rivaled the exploits of the heroes of Wild West thrillers." An African American newspaper, the *Chicago Defender*, raised the race issue in that Dillinger had escaped with a black man. The article was no doubt a jab at the predominant racism of the day.

One of the most eager to hear the news was the escapee's elderly father back on his farm in Mooresville. Although relieved, at the same time John Sr. was worried that his son was on the loose. "It makes a fellow feel a little better," he said, "but of course they may catch him . . . guess I'll start listening to the radio again now. When he was out before, that's about all I did when I wasn't working." While Dillinger's father's interest was personal, Elliot Gorn in his book *Dillinger's Wild Ride* wrote that the American people were "fascinated" by the Hoosier outlaw.

The question being asked across the country about Crown Point was, "How could this have happened?" Political finger pointing, as might be expected, began at once. The Lake County Democrats, who were in charge of the jail, came in for the first round of blame. The competency of Indiana's Democratic governor, Paul V. McNutt, also came under question. If the beleaguered governor could take back one act he had performed since taking office it would no doubt be signing Dillinger's parole. The silver-haired, potential presidential candidate never fully recovered from the fiasco. Yet, his biographer never mentions Dillinger. After his governorship McNutt ended his career as a political appointee in the Philippines and then as a lawyer in Indiana. As might be expected, the Republicans in the state made much of the disaster that had taken place in Crown Point, even distributing wooden guns at political functions. Predictably, Lake County Prosecutor Robert Estill's political career was also over and he was defeated for re-election.

The nationwide publicity the breakout caused quickly caught the attention of the Bureau of Investigation in Washington, D.C. Bureau director J. Edgar Hoover was a political figure in a supposedly nonpolitical position. He had ensured his agency's future and gained personal fame by cracking Great Depression-era bank robberies and kidnappings. While concerned over possible failure, Hoover entered the hunt for Dillinger within a week of the brazen escape. Playing off public indignation, Hoover called the incident an "outrage," going on to say, "Someone is guilty of either nonfeasance or malfeasance. Either negligence or corruption must be at the bottom of this. That is true of nearly all jail breaks. Escape from a good jail is impossible if the jail authorities are both diligent and honest."

Two Crown Point authorities were under investigation. Ernest Blunk, fingerprint expert, and the jailer who had been taken hostage by Dillinger in the breakout, were both questioned, but neither was charged as a grand jury threw the case out. Even Judge William J. Murray came under criticism for not moving Dillinger to Michigan City. There was talk of a film that would be a reenactment of the escape with a wooden gun, but it was never made. Dillinger's fellow Hoosier, Will Hayes, head of the Hayes Commission that regulated and approved all Hollywood productions, declared that "No motion picture based on the life . . . of John Dillinger would be made."

Matt Leach also showed up in Crown Point and complained about Estill's actions. Referring to the photograph with Dillinger, Leach said, "That picture deprived the jail guards of their fear. Love-making [in the 1930s this term meant being unduly friendly] between prosecutors and notorious criminals is shockingly out of place." Neither Leach nor Hoover, however, had any constructive suggestions on what to do next about Dillinger.

The idea of corruption that Hoover had planted in the minds of the American public was increasingly gaining acceptance. A justice in the Criminal Court of Chicago suggested that the escape of thirty convicts from Indiana prisons in the last year could only mean that "graft and corruption existing in many quarters probably also enters into the picture." A U.S. marshal in Chicago also weighed in with his opinion: "This thing is absolutely incredible. There's something wrong with those guards. Even at the risk of their lives they should have prevented his escape." The acting commissioner of the Chicago police delivered a dire warning: "If Dillinger sticks his head inside Chicago he will be shot at first sight. Those are my orders." The city's Dillinger Death Squad leader threatened, "If we do find Dillinger, he'll never go back to Indiana—except in a box!" While criticism came from these four Illinois officials it must be noted that Dillinger had been living in Chicago for the past several months, right under their noses.

Anger continued to be the emotion expressed by most officials. Yet, there remained a certain amount of respect for the man some continued to refer to as "Johnny." A majority of letters to the editors of Indiana newspapers gave Dillinger grudging admiration. One description said that the escape "was marked by desperate courage, unhurried precision, and an occasional laugh for punctuation." The *Crown Point Register* printed the true story that a letter mailed in California to "Harry Meyers, Wooden Gun, Indiana" had been delivered to the city by the U.S. Mail. The idea was floated that the name of Crown Point be changed to "Clown Point" or "Dillinger, Indiana." Other pro-Dillinger sentiment appeared in newspapers, with readers urging McNutt to give the outlaw a pardon and a gold medal, while others said Indiana should be proud of Dillinger, as at least he had brains.

One citizen who did not agree with such public comments was the resident of the White House, Franklin D. Roosevelt. In a radio broadcast the president told the nation he was shocked by the admiration being given a "vicious criminal." Roosevelt called on Americans to "stop romanticizing men who are nothing but insane murderers." On March 19 and 20, 1934, U.S. Attorney General Homer Cummings sent a twelve-point, anticrime program to Congress. Six weeks later he asked Congress for funds to buy airplanes, armored cars, and additional high-powered arms to assist Hoover and his agents. Claire Bond Potter, author of *War on Crime: Bandits, G-Men, and the Politics of Mass Culture*, noted that Dillinger had become "a critical actor in the cultural politics of the New Deal."

The pursuit became a contest between Dillinger and the federal government. The public, whichever side they were rooting for, knew there would be a winner and a loser. After Crown Point the press started to play down Dillinger's danger and play up his easygoing nature—singing as he escaped, ordering his hostage driver not to break the speed limit, and telling the guards he left locked up in the jail to keep their "noses clean." If Dillinger was popular with the press it was because the press found him popular with the public.

Yet the growing number of citizens that had been robbed, shot, and even killed took much of the romanticism out of the outlaw's activities. There was indeed a "Dillinger Legend," but it was tempered by the trail of death and destruction he and other bandits had left in their wake. While some may have liked Dillinger's daring, few may actually have wished to personally meet up with him. One reason given for Dillinger's seemingly effortless escape was fear. When Dillinger pointed a Thompson submachine gun or even a carved toy gun at someone, there was real terror. The sideways grin and cordial manner on his part could turn brutal in the blink of an eye and people who had dealt with Dillinger knew it.

While speculation and editorializing were taking place over the miraculous Crown Point escape, Dillinger and Herbert Youngblood were headed for Chicago. A Chicago detective twice spotted Dillinger the same afternoon he escaped. In the detective's first encounter, he pulled a gun on Dillinger, but then lost him. The second run-in later that night, again by happenstance, ended with Dillinger using his considerable driving skills to lose the unlucky detective in Chicago traffic. The wizard of bank robberies and jailbreaks certainly seemed uncatchable.

Sheriff Lillian Holley's automobile was found two days later on March 5. This was about the only good news, if that could be considered good news, the sheriff received. Crown Point continued to be a hotbed for finger pointing and blame. Estill was hit the hardest as that pesky photograph of him and his prisoner was endlessly reprinted. Unable to say anything more about the episode, Holley decided to say nothing, and it stayed that way for sixty years. Quitting the sheriff's office a month after the escape, she died at the age of 103 in 1994, never again speaking of the Dillinger episode.

While the authorities could not apprehend him, Dillinger had little trouble finding and meeting with his lawyer, Louis Piquett. It has been suggested that Piquett was actually waiting for the phone call from his client, possibly knowing what was going to happen in Crown Point. Piquett met and talked with Dillinger twice the day of the escape. A meeting was held that evening half a block from a police station. "I told him," Piquett later claimed, "that it was impossible for him to defeat the law . . . [and it was] my duty to advise him to surrender." Dillinger's response to his lawyer was that he "would do it later." Maintaining that he was trying his best to bring Dillinger in, Piquett gave the bank robber three hundred dollars and told him where to find his girlfriend, Billie Frechette. The attorney did this although he had yet to be paid anything by Dillinger for legal expenses.

Saying goodbye to his fellow escapee from Crown Point, Dillinger gave Youngblood a hundred dollars. Within weeks Youngblood was killed in a shootout in Michigan. His last act, as he lay dying, was to falsely tell the police Dillinger was in Canada. Dillinger was not in Canada. Neither was he in Missouri, Florida, Texas, Iowa, New York, Oklahoma, or Arizona—all states in which he had supposedly been sighted. Nor was he in Ohio to break out Harry Pierpont, Russell Clark, and Charles Makley. Extra precautions had been taken in Ohio to make sure another breakout did not occur.

Rightly viewing Chicago as too dangerous a place to stay, Dillinger picked up Frechette and headed for Minnesota, arriving in the Twin Cities of Saint Paul and Minneapolis, a day and a half after the breakout in Crown Point. For years Saint Paul had been considered a safe haven for crooks. "Creepy" Karpis, bank robber and kidnapper, once said, "If you were looking for a [criminal of importance] you hadn't seen for a few months, you usually thought of two places—prison or St. Paul." The couple rented an apartment in Minneapolis and was soon back in business.

Business meant putting a new gang together, since most of Dillinger's friends were either in jail or recovering from gunshot wounds. Dillinger was always able to make new contacts and do so with great speed. A new quartet of bandits now joined one of the most famous men in America. The professional bank robbers included old friend Homer Van Meter along with Tommy Carroll, Eddie Green, and Lester Gillis, who was better known by his alias and nickname, George "Baby Face" Nelson.

Nelson was a reform-school alumnus who had been in and out of trouble since he was a kid. Youthful in appearance with a round, chubby face, his looks contradicted his behavior. He was probably the most mentally unbalanced of all the criminals operating at the time. He had a hair-trigger temper, was extremely violent, and completely unpredictable. Some even considered him a "psychopath," a name used at this time for those who were mentally unstable. In spite of his violent lifestyle, as noted earlier, Nelson was a devoted husband with two young children. The very day that Dillinger arrived in Minnesota, Nelson shot and killed a man who "cut him off" while driving on the highway. Nelson trailed the man, who was with his family, got out of the car, and shot him dead.

Nelson later said he acted in self-defense and that the man had chased him.

This new "Second Dillinger Gang," as some called it, wasted no time. At first it seemed that Nelson had recruited and supported Dillinger after his escape. But since the gang was comprised of Van Meter, Carroll, and Green, there was little doubt this was a Dillinger Gang; Nelson was the guest. While the name of the gang never bothered Dillinger or Pierpont, it reportedly did upset Nelson. Within forty-eight hours of getting together the gang was robbing banks.

At 9:50 a.m. on March 6 the new gang slowly drove into Sioux Falls, South Dakota, located several hundred miles west of Saint Paul, and struck the Security National Bank. Because Dillinger had been out of jail less than seventy-two hours, the planning for this job had almost certainly been done by Dillinger's new men. The gang had brought backup, including the now recovered John Hamilton. Two of the gang remained outside and four entered the bank. They were all heavily armed with submachine guns under their long winter coats.

An employee in the Sioux Falls bank, guessing what was going to happen, set off the alarm, unnerving one of the robbers, probably Nelson, who started yelling, "This is a holdup! Everyone on the floor. I'd like to know who set that alarm off. Who did it? Who?" Having jumped onto a marble-topped counter near a window, Nelson saw a motorcycle policeman outside and let loose with a shower of bullets through the window. Although hit four times, the officer lived. "I got one! I got one!" Nelson roared. His reputation for unpredictable behavior was well-deserved. Although there were additional policemen outside, no others attempted to stop the robbery. The well-armed sheriff was afraid to shoot due to the large crowd (estimated at a thousand) assembled outside the bank.

The gang used the familiar exit routine of surrounding themselves with hostages. They had taken five—four women and a man. Several harmless rounds of machine-gun fire were spent in the air, probably by Nelson. The gang piled into the car, putting their "guests" on the running boards of their new Packard. A man took a photograph of the scene and sold it to a national newspaper. The take was a healthy $46,000. A single bullet in the radiator did not stop the Packard's getaway. The sole male hostage was dumped with an insulting crack by one of the holdup men, "Goodbye, shorty, we don't need you anymore." Again, according to routine, roofing nails were thrown out of the windows in case they were being followed by the law. Complaining of the cold, the four women were allowed to get into the car, and to the delight of the men, sat on their laps.

Two police cars with two men each pursued the Packard. Shots

A 1931 mug shot of Lester Gillis, who later won infamy as George "Baby Face" Nelson.

were fired by the lawmen and returned by those in the getaway car. Finally, tired of the chase, gang members stopped the Packard and two or three of the men got out and unloaded on the two police cars. Outgunned and fearing they would hit the female hostages, the lawmen retreated to Sioux Falls. The energized Nelson wanted to chase the police, but the cooler-headed Dillinger yanked him back in the car. The gang next commandeered two cars and moved their guns, loot, and extra gasoline into the new vehicles. They then let the four women hostages go. The women said their captors were well dressed and equally well mannered. Two search airplanes followed the cars from above as they headed back to Saint Paul. Another switch of cars, this one planned, was made and eventually the planes lost contact.

Back in the Twin Cities the men began to count and divide up the money from the Sioux Falls raid. Even hours after the robbery, Nelson remained in a state of high excitement. He insisted on counting the money and Dillinger told him he could. Nelson ended the day as he had behaved throughout it—like a child. Disloyalty was not one of Dillinger's many faults. He used his cut of the South Dakota take to pay Piquett and to funnel funds to Ohio for the defense of Pierpont, Makley, and Clark.

At first some could not believe it had really been Dillinger. How did he do it? Hoover's men did not think it was him and sent only one man to investigate. Those who had witnessed the robbery had little doubt as to the robber's identity. Again, Dillinger quickly captured the nation's attention. Will Rogers was having great fun with the whole episode. Referring to the dismissal of the two jailers blamed for the Crown Point escape, the humorist wrote on March 8, "See where they caught two of the guards that got out of jail with

Dillinger. They had him [Dillinger] surrounded in Chicago, but he robbed a bank in Sioux Falls that day. So they was right on his trail. Just three states behind."

Hoover, Cummings, and Roosevelt saw no humor in what was going on in the Midwest. After the Sioux Falls robbery the Bureau was finally officially looking for Dillinger. On March 7 Melvin Purvis, the chief of the Bureau's Chicago field office, entered the Dillinger case. Using the Dyer Act, a federal law against taking stolen cars across a state line, Purvis gained a warrant for Dillinger. The stolen property was the automobile that belonged to Holley and had crossed from Indiana into Illinois four days earlier. Some have argued that Hoover was still not convinced that putting his newly formed national police force on the case was a good idea. Dillinger was making everyone who went near him look foolish.

Beginning in March 1934 and continuing for the next four months, the lives of Dillinger and Purvis interconnected. While coming close, the two men never actually saw each other face to face until the night of Dillinger's death. Purvis was thirty years old when Hoover called on his special agent in charge in Chicago to lead the Bureau's Dillinger contingent. Having joined the Bureau in 1926, Purvis fit the Hoover profile of a model agent—he was a Southerner, well educated, neatly groomed, good looking, rich, and white. Purvis may have been the one who persuaded Hoover to go after Dillinger. Capturing him would have the potential of giving prestige to the new agency and making a national name for Hoover. The director then, ready or not, became involved in the hunt because he had no other choice.

Purvis was probably ill-prepared for the task to which he had been assigned. In truth, he lacked the basic police training essential for dealing with a criminal of Dillinger's caliber. In addition, Purvis had no contacts or informants in the world of crime. Without these connections he had no real place to begin. Purvis's first attempt to nail a band of crooks was a failure when faulty information led him to the wrong address. This was another embarrassment for all, but especially for Purvis. At times, when it suited him, he joined forces with the Chicago Police Department's Dillinger Death Squad. On March 12 the Bureau published its first wanted poster for Dillinger. The chase had begun.

Dillinger crossed state lines again within a week of the Sioux Falls job. This time, either coming from Minnesota or Illinois, Dillinger and his gang arrived in Iowa. On March 13, the Dillinger gang struck the First National Bank of Mason City, Iowa. There may have been seven men in on this job, but for sure Dillinger, Nelson, Hamilton, Van Meter, Green, and Carroll were present. The day before the robbery two of the gang knocked on the door of a bank cashier's home saying they were looking for an address. Having cased the bank, they did this in order to identify the cashier when the robbery took place.

As the Buick pulled behind the bank, the gang noticed that there was a crew filming a "small town America" feature. Carroll crossed the street and told the cameraman to put his equipment away. "If there's any shooting to be done, we'll do it," said Carroll. When the filmmaker saw the Thompson submachine gun, he speedily packed up his camera. A Dillinger robbery had come very close to being filmed. Rather than go inside as he usually did, Dillinger stayed outside the bank in a supporting role with Nelson by his side.

Green, Hamilton, and Van Meter entered the bank. The three men who were neither as patient nor calm as Dillinger, at first did not seem to know what they were supposed to do. Apparently in doubt, they decided to fire shots from their submachine guns to get everyone's attention. Next the bank president, who had the key to the vault, locked himself in an office. An outraged Van Meter, "acting like a crazy man on the loose" it was later reported, started shooting. The trio began screaming orders to those inside the bank.

Making the robbers' job more difficult, the Mason City bank had recently installed a security cage. Built of bulletproof glass it was located in the lobby fifteen feet above the entrance and occupied by an armed guard. The guard fired a tear-gas canister into Green's back. When this happened, the gang's three inside men turned their attention to the guard in the tower. Forgetting they were there to rob the bank, they began uselessly blasting away at the bulletproof

(Left to right) J. Edgar Hoover, William Stanley, and Melvin Purvis confer at the Justice Department in July 1934.

cage. With the lobby full of customers, the guard decided not to return fire. The confusion increased when a second tear-gas bomb exploded. Customers and robbers kept kicking the tear-gas cans back and forth. When one of the robbers fired into the ceiling, chaos ensued as plaster and dust fell on everyone.

Things were not going much better outside. Nelson had gone into one of his frequent outbursts, firing bullets into the air for no reason. Eventually a bystander was wounded in the leg. The gathering crowd, having earlier seen the movie cameras, believed all the action was part of a Hollywood film. But as more bullets flew, they quickly realized the robbery was for real. Dillinger, still on the outside, got into a gun battle with a policeman hiding behind a rock. The patrolman later declared that Dillinger was not a very good shot, but decided to stay behind the rock. A woman in the bank managed to reach an open back window and yell down to a man standing in the street, "Hey you! Don't you know there is a bank being robbed?" The man was Nelson. He looked up at her and replied, "Are you telling me, lady?"

The cashier, whose home had been visited by the gang, proved to be a sharp adversary. He wasted no time getting into the vault and then the cages inside. Next, he loaded the robbers' sacks with one dollar bills and took his time doing it. The quick-thinking cashier with his stalling tactics saved the bank a vast majority of its holdings. The $52,000 the robbers stole was a fraction of the $250,000 the bank held.

Observing from a third-floor window across the street from the bank, an elderly judge grabbed his antique six-shooter. He fired at Dillinger, hitting him in the shoulder. Although wounded, Dillinger quickly located where the shot had come from and returned a spurt of bullets from his Thompson. The judge with the old gun ducked for cover. Seeing that the situation was deteriorating by the minute, the usually patient Dillinger had had enough and let gang members inside the bank know it was time to go. Taking what money they had, the three men inside gathered the usual party of hostages. As they were going out the door, the old sharpshooter on the third floor fired his gun one more time and again hit his mark. This time it was Hamilton who received a bullet in the shoulder.

Dillinger, who seldom used more force than necessary, was upset when he saw the man Nelson had wounded. When he asked him why he had shot someone for no apparent reason, Nelson said he thought the man was a cop. Parading to their getaway car, the gang had anywhere from thirteen to nineteen hostages. With six, maybe seven, stickup men there could have been as many as twenty-five women and men inside and outside the crooks' vehicle.

Unhappy that a man in a passing car was gawking at the scene, Nelson decided to shoot at him from inside the getaway car. Not giving the hostage on the running board a second thought, he shot right through the man's coat, wounding an unfortunate passerby. With one police car in pursuit and feeling protected with hostages, Nelson ordered the getaway driver to pull over so he could get a better shot. Vetoing his partner's wish to "fight it out with them here," Dillinger told Nelson to get back in the car and threw out the usual roofing nails as they departed. The upset Nelson carelessly threw some under their own car. In exasperation Dillinger told Nelson to get in the backseat, they were leaving. One of the hostages had a bag of sandwiches that for some reason he was holding tightly with his fist. The crooks took the bag from him and enjoyed lunch.

Finally arriving at a gravel pit, the gang shifted into two cars they had hidden and abandoned the hostages. Arriving in Saint Paul, the gang forced a physician at gunpoint to attend to Dillinger and Hamilton. "I'll blow your brains out," the doctor was allegedly told. Hoover had the innocent doctor prosecuted and given a one-year jail term for aiding the criminals.

With the job over, Nelson and his wife decided to head west to Nevada and California. Realizing that the situation was also too hot for him, Dillinger stayed undercover in Saint Paul and sent Frechette on two errands. One was to get $1,000 to his lawyer Piquett and the same amount to Pierpont's attorney. Frechette asked Piquett and his associate to complete her divorce and if he knew a plastic surgeon. Her "Johnnie" wanted some work done on his face. Piquett said he did not do divorces. His associate went looking for the plastic surgeon. After dealing with Piquett, Frechette's next task was to get money to Dillinger's family in Indiana.

Placing Frechette on an American Airways flight from Chicago to Indianapolis, Dillinger sent money with her for his family and the famous Crown Point wooden gun for his sister, Audrey Hancock. A letter from Dillinger to his sister said, "Don't worry about me . . . I am having a lot of fun." Referring to the gun, he said that pulling off the escape with the carved piece of wood "was worth ten years of my life. Don't part with my wooden gun for any price." From the Crown Point interview to letters to his family and later photographs, he played the part the media was creating for him. Dillinger told his sister he would get back to Mooresville when things cooled off and buy her and his father new cars. He closed with, "I got shot a week ago but I'm all right now. Just a little sore. Lots of love from Johnnie."

Her business finished, Frechette boarded a plane in Indianapolis and returned safely to Chicago. Officials there were on the lookout for her. Unfortunately in early April they misidentified a woman thought to be Frechette. Acting on an erroneous tip the Bureau held Betty Marx, the wife of Chico Marx of the comedic Hollywood Marx Brothers, for questioning. She accepted an apology for the mistaken identity and the G-men once again looked foolish. (G-Man was the shortened name for government man. According to the Bureau of Investigation history, the term was coined by George "Machine Gun" Kelly.)

While Frechette was in Mooresville, Dillinger may have made a trip to Ohio to visit Pierpont's parents. There were rumors that Dillinger was coming for his pals in Ohio, but this was not going to happen. Steps had been taken to prevent a breakout. Ohio National Guard units were in place and the jail was ringed by barbed wire. Machine-gun nests were on the ground as well as on the roofs of nearby buildings. An eight-foot fence surrounded the sheriff's residence. The money sent to the Pierpont family for legal assistance did no good. Pierpont and Makley were convicted of first-degree murder and sentenced to the electric chair. Clark was given life imprisonment.

On March 27 the three prisoners were moved from Lima, Ohio, to the state prison in Columbus. There were forty-five armed guards in the caravan and two truckloads of Ohio National Guardsmen. Dillinger never had a realistic chance of springing his buddies. The three prisoners had even changed into good clothes in preparation for Dillinger freeing them. But Makley, for one, knew there would be no rescue. Referring to the electric chair, he said, "I'd rather take the hot squat than see Johnnie caught."

March ended with Dillinger and Frechette in Minneapolis. They spent their time buying Dillinger another new car, Frechette more clothes, and going to the movies. One evening a newsreel before the movie featured stories of the Sioux Falls and Mason City robberies, John Sr. appeared on the screen saying, "John isn't a bad boy. They're trying to make a mountain out of a molehill. They ought to give him a chance. He just robbed some banks." Dillinger looked on in amusement, even laughing, until Frechette told him he was drawing attention to himself. But for the most part, Dillinger and Frechette kept a very low profile—window shades were drawn, meals were eaten in the apartment, and they always left by the building's back door. Frechette did draw looks from teenage boys when she hung laundry to dry wearing shorts and a halter top. The boys whistled at her and then ran away.

Instead of shielding them from scrutiny, the couple's behavior did just the opposite. Their secretive way of life made their landlady suspicious. On March 30 she telephoned the Bureau informing it that there was a couple in the building that seemed shifty. The next day two federal agents and a local Saint Paul police detective arrived at the Dillinger apartment. They knocked on the door and asked for Carl, the name Dillinger had been using.

Frechette later told what happened next: "I said he was not at home. I asked the men who they were, and they said, 'We are police. Can we come in and talk with you?' I said I was sorry but I was not dressed and told them to wait a minute. John asked me who the men were and kept saying, 'Hurry up and get dressed' and 'Never mind, never mind.' I heard some shots. John started shooting through the door and I shouted to him, 'Don't shoot! Try and get out without shooting! He kept yelling, 'Come on, let's go!'"

At this point, with one agent pinned down, the other agent went to the rear stairway to make sure their suspects did not escape out the back. The local police officer called for backup, which never arrived. The agent heading down the backstairs ran into Dillinger's friend Van Meter coming up the stairs to visit Dillinger. Smiling, he told the agent he was a soap salesman. The agent asked to see samples of the products salesmen usually carried with them. Van Meter said they were in his car. By the time the federal agent reached the ground floor, he found Van Meter standing in a basement doorway with a revolver leveled at him. The two men immediately exchanged shots. Going out the backdoor, Van Meter left his car behind and jumped onto a horse-drawn garbage wagon, grabbing the driver's hat. When out of sight, he jumped off the cart, keeping the driver's cap as a disguise.

Back at the apartment Dillinger was having his own gun battle with the other agent. Sticking his submachine gun out the apartment door and down the narrow hallway, he was firing off bursts as Frechette packed their suitcases with clothes and guns. In the exchange of fire, Dillinger had been hit in the leg, accidently shooting himself when one of his own bullets ricocheted off a wall. Bleeding, he and Frechette made it to the garage, got into their new Terraplane, and sped away. The agents did not follow. Surprised and seemingly surrounded, Dillinger had escaped again.

What Dillinger and Frechette left behind in their apartment proved to be of great value to the Bureau. First, they were able to identify the couple through fingerprints. They also abandoned a full set of armaments—two automatic rifles, a .38-caliber Colt automatic with twenty-shot magazine clips, and bulletproof vests. Personal items that Frechette left included an array of nightgowns, underwear, a wig, shoes, slacks, and dresses. Dillinger had not had time to pack a closetful of clothes, a silk bathrobe, and several photographs of himself. A road map was also discovered giving exact directions on how to get to Saint Paul from Iowa without going through any towns. The agents thus discovered that placing roadblocks on major highways was a waste of time. Most important the fleeing felons had left a slip of paper with one of Dillinger's associate's (Green's) telephone numbers.

After their escape Dillinger and Frechette drove to Green's house. Green took Dillinger to a shady physician who was promised $500 to patch Dillinger up. In the end the doctor was never paid. Threatened with death, "I'll blow your brains out if you do anything about this," the doctor drove Dillinger to the apartment of his nurse and treated the outlaw there. Green helped Dillinger at the cost of his life. Using the phone number found in the Dillinger apartment, federal agents were able to track Green to his house. In a shootout, Green was struck in the back and seriously wounded.

Green survived for a week in the hospital. During this time, agents pumped him for information about Dillinger. Moving in and out of consciousness, Green unknowingly gave out the names of the two doctors who treated Dillinger and Hamilton and the identities of the gang that had robbed the Sioux Falls and Mason City banks. Green also divulged that Dillinger was considering plastic surgery. The questioning of a wounded and dying suspect by federal agents was criticized in the pages of the *Saint Paul Dispatch*. Embarrassed, Hoover retaliated by feeding information to a rival Saint Paul newspaper. The Bureau's assistant director was sent from Washington to follow up on the case, assigning agents to the address Green had divulged. The apartment was raided.

Unfortunately it was the correct address but the wrong apartment. Dillinger had actually been recovering downstairs and had left the day before. Once again, he had escaped barely in the nick of time.

March of 1934 had ended an extraordinary month for Dillinger. He had escaped jail, taken part in two robberies, had a shootout with federal agents, and been wounded twice in a little over three weeks. Most importantly, he continued to appear to the public as untouchable by the authorities. And those authorities—from federal to state to local—seemed incapable of doing anything right. April would be a new month. Surely the luck of the agents and police would change. Or so they hoped.

8

Catch Me if You Can

The bungled attempt to capture John Dillinger in Saint Paul, Minnesota, in March 1934, was more than J. Edgar Hoover in Washington, D.C., could handle. At this point Hoover decided to increase the resources he had at his disposal. Cautious over becoming part of the failed attempts to capture Dillinger, Hoover's game had been not to lose rather than to win. This now changed. One observer called Hoover's new crusade to track Dillinger down "relentless." In early April 1934 Hoover sent fifty agents to the Twin Cities under the leadership of his two assistant Bureau directors. Using the phrase "War on Crime," Hoover was going after not only Dillinger, but also Baby Face Nelson, Pretty Boy Floyd, Ma Barker's Gang, and even Bonnie and Clyde, although the Texas couple were nowhere close to Minnesota.

A genuine sighting of Dillinger occurred in early April. He was in Mooresville, Indiana, for a brief visit to his father's farm. On April 4 he and Billie Frechette arrived in Indiana. While Dillinger hid in the barn with the car, Frechette knocked on the farmhouse door. John Sr. and Frechette had never met. The elder Dillinger thought her young, pretty, and with dark skin that looked "foreign." He had her bring his son into the house, warning them both it was not safe. "Probably not, Dad, but I just wanted to see you before," Dillinger

paused before going on, "well, you know, before anything happens."
Actually the house was only being watched on and off by various
lawmen. Dillinger told his family that Frechette was his wife and
that her name was Anne. Calling his son "Johnnie my boy," father
and son hugged, Dillinger in an expensive suit and his father in
a nightshirt and slippers. When his half brother Hubert arrived,
Dillinger jumped out from behind a door with his finger pointed
like a gun and said, "Stick 'em up!"

Frechette stayed on the farm while Dillinger and Hubert drove
to Ohio to meet with Harry Pierpont's family. The fate of his former
gang members was always on Dillinger's mind. The two men painted
the trim and wheels of the Hudson Terraplane black to match the
rest of the car. The bright yellow wheels made the automobile too
easy to identify. When they got to Ohio they found that Pierpont's
family had moved to northern Indiana. The trip wasted, the two
men returned to Indiana. It proved to be a risky trip when Hubert
fell asleep at the wheel of the Terraplane, sideswiping a Model-T
Ford in Noblesville, north of Indianapolis. Promising to return to
pay for the damages, Dillinger hid in a haystack with his machine
gun three miles from the scene of the accident. Hubert hitchhiked
back to Indianapolis, retrieved his own car, and quickly went back
to pick up his half brother.

Finding the Terraplane the next day the county sheriff called
Indiana State Police captain Matt Leach in Indianapolis. Leach
had been idle for several weeks while the Dillinger Gang had been
operating outside of his state. Tracing the license plate back to
Minnesota, he was able to connect the car to Dillinger. Leach noted
that the field where the automobile had landed was full of stumps,
but it had not struck one of them. While Leach never seemed to

have any luck at all, he commented that "Dillinger's Luck" was still holding. The outlaw had made another successful getaway. Leach, knowing Dillinger must certainly be back in central Indiana, placed officers to watch the Dillinger family's farm, the brother-in-law's gas station in Indianapolis, and sister Audrey's home in Maywood. The Bureau also sent men to watch these locations.

When Dillinger returned to the farm in Mooresville after his adventure in the haystack, he sent Frechette to buy a new car. Unable to locate a new Hudson Terraplane, Dillinger's car of choice, she settled on a black Ford V-8. She paid $725 for it with ten-dollar bills and the new car was hidden in a garage in town. With the automobile business taken care of, it was time for a real family reunion, which was held on Sunday, April 8. The gathering was quite large and included Audrey and Dillinger's niece, Mary Hancock.

Although police and federal agents were watching the home place, they still did not know that Dillinger was there. It turned out that several neighbors did know he was there, but, as usual, none of them turned him in. "When the word was out that John was home, all the state cops would come," a neighbor remembered. "But they were so afraid of him they used to put their sirens on five miles away and John Dillinger had time to dig a hole and bury himself. We'd hear 'em coming and say, 'John's home.' We figured they wanted John to know they were coming." A joke in Mooresville was that the road in front of the Dillinger farm had been widened so Dillinger could arrive and leave faster.

There seemed to be no attempt to keep the visit secret as the family, about a dozen relatives in all, had Sunday dinner outside. The menu included two of Dillinger's favorite foods, fried chicken and coconut-cream pie. Gathering on the lawn was thought to be

Dillinger shows off his weapons during a visit to his family's farm in Mooresville, Indiana.

safer than being indoors. An airplane did fly low over the house, but it was identified as an Indiana National Guard training flight. "John was as relaxed as anyone could be," Audrey recalled. "He never seemed concerned except when the airplane pulled over."

Audrey said that her brother talked in detail about the Crown Point escape: "He made a sketch and told us every move he made, then burned the paper up. He told us he took a razor blade and whittled the top part of the gun, then blackened it and drilled a hole in the end and put in a piece out of the safety razor so it looked like a pistol." Dillinger shared stories about his exploits with family members but only up to a point. When his brother-in-law started to quiz him, he turned very serious and said, "Big boy, let me tell you something. If you don't know anything you can't tell anything, can you?" There were no more questions. It was on this day that a famous photograph of Dillinger was taken. Standing outside his father's farmhouse he held a machine gun in one hand and the Crown Point jail wooden gun in the other.

Mary, the outlaw's favorite niece, believed the law knew her uncle was at the farm, but had decided not to have a gunfight in front of the family. She remembered the two of them taking a walk and Dillinger telling her, "You can believe what's in the papers if you want to, but take it from me, I haven't killed anyone and I never will." She was wrong, though, about the lawmen not being ready to take Dillinger if they had the chance. One nearby resident said, "The FBI was around constantly. They had headquarters in Mooresville."

John Sr. had bleaker memories of the homecoming. While his son was indeed carefree, laughing often that afternoon, there was also a sense of foreboding in him. "He'd seen a lot of the country, and he'd got even, and he sensed he was going to die," said John Sr.

Dilliger told his father, "I've set my course and I'll have to follow it to the end. I will never go back to prison alive." The two men also took a long walk that afternoon. His father asked, "John, if anything happens to you, what do you want me to do? I've got room for you at Crown Hill [cemetery] right next to your mother." Dillinger looked up and said, "That'll be all right, Dad." Knowing that the chase might soon be over, Dillinger realized that this was probably his final visit. With the brief family reunion over, Frechette and Dillinger decided it was time to leave.

The new Ford was retrieved from Mooresville by a relative and departed the farm about four o'clock Sunday afternoon. Frechette drove while Dillinger took cover in the backseat under a blanket. His sister and niece were also in the car. With Dillinger hiding, it appeared that three women were out for a Sunday drive. Two other cars left the Dillinger farm. At the same time two new federal agents were cruising back and forth near the Dillinger place. One of the relatives left driving a green Chevrolet and the rookie Bureau agents decided to follow it. Eventually losing the Chevy, the agents headed back to the farm.

Upon their return, they noticed the new Ford parked by the roadside, saw the three women, and noted a nicely dressed man in his early thirties getting out of the car. Dillinger had stopped to stretch, put on a pair of sunglasses, and take over driving. The two agents looked at him, but drove right by. Because they were so new on the job they did not have a description of Dillinger and so did not recognize him. The family reunion had been a success. Fourteen federal agents raided the Dillinger farm later that day. They thought of arresting John Sr., but cooler heads prevailed in Washington, D.C. Arresting a seventy-year-old man might make the Bureau look like bullies.

The Bureau was again just a little too late. That evening after
Dillinger left Mooresville, a half dozen federal agents moved into a
nearby farmhouse, placing John Sr.'s homestead under surveillance.
They dressed like farmhands, working the fields and mending fences,
in the hopes of not attracting attention. The visit and escape proved
two points. First, Dillinger seemed able to outsmart those chasing
him, even the Bureau. Second, the fact that no one "gave him up"
showed that there appeared to be sympathy for the outlaw. Headlines
in newspapers soon read, "Dillinger is Regarded as Hero in Old Home
Town" and "Dillinger Given Warm Welcome in Home Town."

The reaction in Mooresville was mixed. Some citizens were
not especially proud of their local celebrity bandit. Town officials
preferred to focus on the hardworking, churchgoing John Sr. On
the other hand a Mooresville Bank had recently closed, a victim
of the Great Depression. As townspeople were losing their hard-
earned money, a few felt it was alright if "Johnnie," one of their
own, was getting a little back from the banks. One neighbor, who
hid Dillinger's car for him, was asked by a federal agent if he had
also let the fugitive sleep on the floor of his house. "Why, I would
have given him my bed," the man replied.

Dillinger's hometown even petitioned the governor to pardon
the outlaw. "I wouldn't be afraid if John walked in here right now,"
said a Mooresville banker. "He's a town boy and I don't think he
would hurt any of us. We don't even take any precautions against
him!" A similar attempt for amnesty had been tried by citizens of
Missouri in the previous century. In that case, it was an appeal on
behalf of Jesse James. The connection to James, whom Dillinger
had read about as a youth, was made by *Time* magazine. Both
men, the magazine claimed, had the traits of honor, leadership,

and bravery. Later it would be noted that both men were shot in the back.

The Mooresville newspaper ran a story with large headlines reading DILLINGER ATTENDS FAMILY REUNION IN THE MIDST OF MANHUNT. John Sr. was interviewed and the always honest farmer told reporters, "Oh, yes, John came down here to look in on me. He was hurt in the leg a little, but not much. I don't aim to tell no lies, even to keep things like that quiet. I didn't tell the police because they didn't ask me. John's not in Indiana now." State police officials were stunned that Mooresville protected the high-profile criminal. "It is unusual for a community to withhold such information for days and then let it reach the newspapers in such a way that it disparages the police," said one officer. "I simply can't understand it." Leach said he would not question Dillinger's father. "What good would it do?" he asked. "Dillinger's been and gone, and under the law the old man has the right to protect his son." The senior Dillinger did refuse several hundred dollars to go on the road and give talks about his famous offspring.

A journalist who visited Mooresville after the famous weekend visit found that some in town thought Dillinger was a pretty good guy. Asking a gas station attendant's opinion, the man replied, "You could have talked to him yourself right here about ten days ago. He came in to get gas and have his oil changed." "After he broke out of Crown Point?" asked the surprised journalist. "Sure," said the attendant. "He stayed with his old man two days." A banker told a similar story. Incredulous, the magazine writer asked, "You mean to say that the most-wanted criminal in America could stroll around here in his home town, eighteen miles from Indianapolis, without anybody turning him in?" The banker replied, "Nobody ever did."

Defense attorney Clarence Darrow won fame through his actions in such notable cases as the Scopes Monkey Trial and the murder trial of Nathan Leopold and Richard Loeb for the thrill killing of fourteen-year-old Robert "Bobby" Franks in 1924.

As usual, when no one had actually seen Dillinger for several days, sightings of him became common. It made for good copy in the newspapers. There was a John Dillinger Fan Club. Some joked he should run for governor of Indiana. His ability to elude capture became humorous to many. One unfortunate man named Ralph Alsman lived in Brookville, Indiana, and was a dead ringer for Dillinger. He had been picked up seventeen times by the spring of 1934 and was in fear of the rumored "shoot-to-kill" order out on his "twin."

A newsreel company offered a $5,000 reward for Dillinger's capture. A gossip columnist wrote that an unnamed movie star wanted to hire detectives to find Dillinger so that the actor could be filmed capturing him. The *Christian Century* labeled the outlaw a "lethal and social menace" and thought he was being given too much attention. Others defended him. The most famous defense attorney in the United States, Clarence Darrow, said the cause of Dillinger's difficulties was that unfair sentence meted out a decade before. Darrow did not think Dillinger should be sentenced to life if caught and strongly disagreed with the rumors that the government had shoot-to-kill orders out on the bank robber.

The entrance of the federal government in the hunt for Dillinger did make it a new game. On Monday, April 9, Dillinger and Frechette arrived in Chicago. Needing a place to stay they had made arrangements to meet a possible contact at a downtown bar. They may have missed him in Minnesota and Indiana, but Bureau agents were waiting for Dillinger in the Windy City. Lead agent Melvin Purvis brought a dozen men with him. Dillinger usually had a keen sense of danger when it came to possible traps, but this time he suspected nothing out of the ordinary. Fortunately for him Frechette did. For some reason she thought the meeting might be a "set-up." She was correct, federal agents were waiting in the bar. Thinking back to what had occurred in Tucson, Arizona, she said to Dillinger, "I'll go in. The last time you went in somewhere you were arrested." Entering the tavern she was immediately seized by the agents. When asked how she arrived at the bar, Frechette lied and said a taxi. They believed her.

Since agents were also outside the tavern it is remarkable that they did not see Dillinger drop Frechette off. One or two agents ran right past the black Ford with the man they were looking for sitting inside. Another one was within five feet of Dillinger's car and failed to recognize him. The car slowly pulled away from the curb and drove around the block a few times. With a Thompson in his lap, Dillinger was waiting for a chance to rescue Frechette. More police arrived and she was placed in a squad car. Dillinger knew any attempt to liberate her would fail. He later said that as he saw her taken away he cried like a baby. He next called his attorney, Louis Piquett, telling him "the whiskers grabbed Billie" and asked him to defend her; Piquett agreed to do so.

Bureau agents took Frechette to their offices in the Bankers Building. Reportedly, the treatment was fairly rough. Frechette alleged that she was "called a 'Dirty Indian,' kicked in my stomach, had my hair pulled, and slapped in my face to get me to tell them where he [Dillinger] was." She was not allowed to sleep and finally a secretary intervened with Purvis to ease up on her. Agreeing with his secretary, he allowed Frechette some sleep, but then put her back under the bright lights for more questioning. There was never any evidence that Purvis had personally mistreated Frechette in any way, but others may have. When Dillinger later heard about all this he threatened to kill the agents.

Frechette kept her silence but did taunt the agents with stories. Dillinger had been in the bar with her and they had missed him, she told them, a statement Purvis called "ridiculous." She sent them on a wild goose chase, saying Dillinger and she had planned to meet in the city. When agents came back empty-handed she said they were incompetent. "Watch out for John," she told the agents, "he's a big bad wolf you know." In the end, she never broke and the Bureau failed to get any information from her. Capturing Billie was a coup for the Bureau and Hoover reportedly told Purvis, "Now get Dillinger for me and the world is yours."

By all accounts, Dillinger was extremely upset about Frechette's capture. How to rescue her (as well as his friends in jail in Ohio) consumed him. He planned to gain her freedom when she was transferred to Saint Paul, Minnesota. Eventually, Dillinger was convinced that he would not be able to help Frechette. The odds were against him and he did not have the manpower for a major gunfight. Piquett traveled to Saint Paul to defend her. To help his friends, Dillinger was going to need more money, meaning another bank job. Knowing it would be risky, Dillinger decided to obtain additional guns and bulletproof vests.

On April 13 Dillinger and Homer Van Meter arrived in Warsaw, Indiana, a medium-sized community in the north-central part of the state. A night patrolman at the police station related what happened next: "They asked me how many officers were on duty at night and I told them four, although there really were only two of us. I tried to scare them by saying I expected the other three along soon. They demanded the keys to the room where the guns were kept. I tried to stall, but finally opened it." Another version of the story has Van Meter beating the policeman until Dillinger stopped him. The duo made off with two guns and several bulletproof vests. "America's No.1 vanishing outlaw has vanished again," wrote one newspaper. Another added that, as usual, "He left no forwarding address."

Some of the best firsthand information on Dillinger's movements at this time comes from G. Russell Girardin of Chicago, who signed an agreement with Piquett and the attorney's associate, Arthur O'Leary, to write a series of magazine articles in 1936 and 1937 titled "Dillinger Speaks." The manuscript and its author were later discovered by William Helmer, an expert on outlaws between World War I and World War II. Helmer added context to the Girardin material and the men coauthored a book titled *Dillinger: The Untold Story*. Most of the information in the book comes from two men, Piquett and O'Leary, whose truthfulness has been questioned. Even with this material from two men very close to Dillinger, there were

A front view of the Little Bohemia Lodge in April 1934 following the botched raid by federal agents to capture the Dillinger gang.

still days in which his presence was unaccounted for.

By April 17 Dillinger was on the road to Sault Ste. Marie, Michigan, with John Hamilton. The purpose of the trip was to drop off a new Ford for Hamilton's sister. He too, as with Dillinger's reunion in Mooresville, felt the need to make a final family visit. The stay was brief as federal agents were on their trail. The lawmen again arrived two days late, but punished Hamilton's sister and her seventeen-year-old son through fines and brief jail terms. A gas-station attendant in Michigan recognized Dillinger, but thinking it could not really be him failed to call the police. After the Michigan jaunt with Hamilton, the Hoosier outlaw again vanished without a trace.

After spending some time in Chicago on April 18 and 19, the Dillinger Gang decided that it needed to cool off a bit. Dillinger was also still recovering from the wounds he had received the previous month. The gang chose, therefore, to spend some time in the isolated woods of northern Wisconsin. Called the Little Bohemia Lodge by its owner, Emil Wanatka, it was located thirteen miles south of Mercer, Wisconsin. Mid-April weather was still cold in the northlands, but the lodge had remained open. Wanatka was trying hard to keep his out-of-the-way hotel and restaurant financially afloat. Opened in 1930 Little Bohemia was a two-story structure with a dining room, bar, kitchen, and a large room with a fireplace on the first floor. The guest rooms were located upstairs. There was also a set of cabins along one side of the lodge. It was a good choice for the gang in that it sat off the road and was completely hidden in a heavy growth of dense trees. Behind the lodge was a lake with a concealed beach.

On Friday April 20, the first of the gang arrived. Van Meter, Pat Reilly, and his girlfriend asked if Wanatka could put up a dozen guests for two or three days. Wanatka jumped at the chance to rent out that many rooms in the off-season. Garages, always important in terms of getaways, were also available. Later that afternoon two other cars arrived. They carried Dillinger, Hamilton and Tommy Carroll with their girlfriends, and Baby Face Nelson and his wife, Helen. When two of the resort employees carried the groups' bags into the lodge one remarked to the other, "There must be lead in this one. What are these guys, hardware salesmen?"

Dillinger and Reilly roomed together in the main building, where the Hamilton couple also stayed. The rest of the gang, a total of six men and four women, was located in the cottages. Wanatka's wife first became suspicious when Nelson told her that his wife would be cleaning the rooms for the entire party—both in the cottages and upstairs in the lodge. Frightened, she told her husband, "I don't want them to stay." This was before she even knew their true identities. That evening, Wanatka played cards, poker, with the gang. Dillinger, whom Wanatka called Johnnie, beat him in the final hand. He called his guest "a good card player and a genial fellow." During a card game Wanatka noticed the men were carrying guns in shoulder holsters under their suit coats.

In the lodge there was a Chicago newspaper carrying a photograph of Dillinger. Seeing it, Wanatka was now able to identify his guest. After a sleepless night and an irritatingly long breakfast with the gang, Wanatka said to Dillinger, "Johnnie, could I talk to you?" Dillinger agreed and the two men entered a small office. "Emil, what's wrong? What do you want?" asked Dillinger. Wanatka looked him in the eye and said, "You're John Dillinger." Gazing back at Wanatka, he said calmly, "You're not afraid, are you?" Wanatka said no, adding he was not interested in a "shooting match" in his lodge or with his family present. Dillinger patted Wanatka on the shoulder and said, "All we want is to eat and rest for a few days. We'll pay you well and get out. There won't be any trouble."

The situation, at least for that day, seemed to settle down. After breakfast the gang decided to take target practice. Wanatka did not think the gang, except for Van Meter, were very good shots. Dillinger played pinochle with Wanatka, who later claimed to have cheated his guest. Wanatka's son, Emil Jr., played catch with Dillinger for a while and then Nelson joined in. Emil Jr. finally quit because Nelson, always a bully except with his own kids, threw the baseball much too hard at the youngster. This was all too much for Wanatka's wife, who took her son to a neighbor's house. Another boy visiting the lodge for the day noticed Dillinger's dyed red hair. "Why does the nice man have different color hair than his eyebrows?" he asked, but he never received an answer.

Things were not calm among the gang members. Old rivalries reemerged as Nelson, tense and temperamental, became offended over imagined slights. These included Dillinger being given a room in the lodge, while he and his wife were in a cottage, and the old problem of the press referring to the "Dillinger Gang." Civility was important to Dillinger and if Nelson had asked nicely, he would have been given the better room. He put up with Nelson in part because Baby Face had included him in the Sioux Falls robbery. Having just escaped from Crown Point and in need of cash, Nelson had cut Dillinger in on the job. But he knew he could push Dillinger only so far.

Nelson did not like the risks that Dillinger seemed to take, and Dillinger and the rest of the gang thought Baby Face volatile and mentally unbalanced. Having him as part of the gang was not a popular decision. The only professional credentials that seemed to matter to Dillinger, however, were results. And most of the time, when a job was over, Nelson had delivered. Like him or not, the gang decided to keep him around. But that did not mean that the two men trusted each other.

There were actually more important issues for the gang to be concerned about and they knew it. Once Wanatka had recognized Dillinger, the rest of the men became extremely guarded. When anyone entered the driveway, the gang asked Wanatka about them. They also listened closely to all phone calls that came in and went out. Nelson followed Wanatka's wife when she took her son to the neighbor's home. Although they did not know it at the time, the gang was smart to be vigilant. The Wanatkas were planning to rid the lodge of their unwanted guests with the help of the law.

Through a series of coded phone calls, phony trips to town, and even messages passed in packages of cigarettes, the Wanatkas sent word to family in a nearby town about their unwelcome lodgers. The relatives contacted a U.S. marshal in Chicago who on Sunday, April 22, got in touch with Purvis. That Sunday afternoon Purvis was taking a rare day off. Agents, considered on duty around the clock, seven days a week, had to let someone know where they were every hour. The phone rang in Purvis's apartment and a voice said, "The man you want most is up here." "You mean Dillinger?" asked Purvis. "Six members of the Dillinger gang are at a resort called Little Bohemia and John Dillinger is one of them," came the response. Purvis, believing the tip important, immediately called Washington, D.C. Hoover decided to put Assistant Bureau Director Hugh Clegg in charge of the operation. Clegg was close by in Saint

Paul. Purvis then chartered two six-passenger airplanes for his agents and himself that very Sunday afternoon. He also called in agents from Duluth, Minnesota, and Milwaukee, Wisconsin.

The flight from Chicago to Wisconsin was bumpy and some of the agents had never flown before. Purvis and his men arrived outfitted with machine guns, tear gas, pistols, and bulletproof vests. They did not know exactly what was going to happen, but knew whatever was to take place had the potential to be big. It would indeed turn out to be big—big trouble for the agents that is. Purvis had been informed by Wanatka that the gang was going to be at the lodge at least through Monday night. On Sunday morning, though, Dillinger informed Wanatka that the gang would be leaving on Monday morning, April 23. He paid the owner a generous five hundred dollars for the group's brief stay and told his host how nice everything had been.

Finding out they did not have an extra day, Clegg and Purvis decided that the agents had no choice but to storm the lodge Sunday night. Never having seen the lodge, they were at a disadvantage from the start. They were also unsure how many outlaws they would encounter. Preparation for the raid was therefore impossible. That was only the beginning of their problems. Arriving in Rhinelander, Wisconsin, at 5:00 p.m., they were still fifty miles from Little Bohemia. Needing cars for seventeen men they finally secured five cars—three rentals and two taxis. Two vehicles broke down and eight agents had to ride standing on the running boards of the remaining three autos in the frigid Wisconsin night. They reached the lodge at 9:00 p.m.

At Little Bohemia a Sunday night dollar dinner special was being served. Surprisingly about seventy-five customers had arrived.

Dillinger and his gang mixed with the dinner guests. By the end of the evening only three patrons, all men, were left in the lodge. The hastily put-together plan was for five federal agents in bulletproof vests to attack the lodge from the front, while the others flanked to the left and right. With the lake in back of the lodge as a barrier, it seemed the spur-of-the-moment strategy just might work. Most of the agents were not trained for a raid in an unknown location with some of the nation's most dangerous men. As the men approached the lodge in the dark, Wantaka's two dogs began barking, yet no one inside seemed to notice. Then everything went terribly wrong.

The three last men to finish their Sunday night dinner left the lodge, got into a Chevrolet, and turned on the radio. Unfortunately for them they enjoyed their music loud. They were leaving just as the agents were ready to make their charge toward the lodge. The three men in the Chevrolet, forgetting to turn their lights on and the volume of their radio down, headed straight for the waiting agents. Machine guns ready, the agents began yelling, "Halt, we're federal officers!" Not hearing the warning due to the music from the radio, they kept driving. Believing the car was making a getaway with the crooks inside, the agents decided to start shooting. Purvis's Thompson seemed to jam (no expert with firearms, he had actually forgotten to take the safety off) and so he reached for his .45. The other agents then opened fire on the Chevy and all three men inside the car were hit. One passenger who jumped from the car, when asked to identify himself, truthfully gave the unfortunate answer, "John." The "wrong John," not Dillinger, then headed for the lake behind the cabins and lodge. The second passenger fell to the ground, and the third man, behind the steering wheel, was dead. The Chevrolet was riddled with almost thirty bullet holes as its radio continued to blare in the cold night air. "It was like a big windstorm," one of the men said later of the assault on the car.

Two employees stepped back inside the lodge and shouted to the agents, "Don't shoot! Those are customers of ours!" Wanatka and his two employees went directly to the basement with three women. When the bullets began flying Dillinger swiftly left the card table and moved upstairs. His keen sense for trouble was highly tuned. Some have reported that there was an extended gun battle involving the agents in the trees with Dillinger and Hamilton. He briefly returned fire toward the agents, then made his way out the back through a second-floor window. Dillinger and Hamilton, joined by Van Meter, went toward the lakefront which was several feet below the lodge. The drop-off gave the bad guys cover from the agents in the front of the lodge. Not knowing the lay of the land, Purvis and his men never saw the three men escape.

Outside the lodge a real gun battle had begun as Nelson and Carroll returned the agents' fire. Nelson, however, wisely decided to end the gunfight and slip off around the lake and into the dark, leaving his wife behind. Some of the agents got entangled in barbed wire near the cottages and took no part in the gun battle. Other agents stumbled into a drainage ditch. With his men either confused or lost, Purvis had little chance to take the lodge.

Returning from Saint Paul, Reilly and his female companion drove right into the middle of the pitched gun battle. Reilly quickly turned off his headlights and reversed out of the driveway as agents began firing at him. For some reason the couple returned to the lodge. They were fired upon again and this time a tire was hit. The woman fell part way out of the car, was pulled back in by Reilly, then was struck in her cheek by a bullet. He also backed the car into a tree before managing to escape on three tires.

Wanatka and his employees ran out of his lodge and mistakenly told Purvis and his agents that the outlaws were still inside. Purvis and Clegg, the agent Hoover had put in charge, decided to wait until dawn and then clear the building with tear gas. The three women remained in the basement of the lodge, a fact Wanatka failed to tell Purvis. As the agents waited Dillinger and his gang made their getaway. The agents had made a number of mistakes—they did not have a plan, they shot at cars unsure who was in them, incorrectly thought Dillinger and his friends were still in the lodge, and decided to wait until dawn to make their next move. Hoover may have been right that his agency was not ready to deal with the likes of Dillinger.

Two agents left the lodge in pursuit of Reilly and drove right into the arms of Nelson, who was trying to start a car he had stolen. A voice yelled, "Halt! We're federal officers." Nelson yelled back, "I'll kill you. Get out of that car." One of the agents got out and reached for his gun. That was all the excuse Nelson needed. He jumped out of the car with his gun blazing—a Colt .45 that had been altered into a machine gun. Spewing profanities, he shrieked he knew the agents were wearing vests and would be aiming for their heads. He hit one agent near his eye and another in the neck, where the bullet went down into his chest, killing him. The other agent who had been shot by Nelson had wounds in the lungs, liver, chest, hip, arm and ankle. Amazingly he recovered.

Meanwhile, back at the lodge Wanatka left to go to a neighbor's house for help. Witnessing the bloodshed Wanatka ran back to the lodge, where agents almost shot him. "Don't shoot! It's Emil Wanatka!" he shouted. At this point Purvis decided to become a bureaucrat rather than a lawman. Having heard Wanatka's name that afternoon in the Chicago phone call, Purvis asked him how to spell both his name and the name of the town Manitowish. Wanatka erupted. "All your men are dead. Did you come here to get Dillinger or me?" Realizing this information was not that important, Purvis then asked where the shooting had taken place. After telling Purvis, the lodge owner borrowed a truck, removed the victim from the Chevrolet, and drove the dying man for help. By the time Wanatka arrived at the nearby Civilian Conservation Corps camp the man was dead.

While Nelson was on his rampage, Dillinger, Hamilton, and Van Meter made their way in the dark to another resort about a mile from Little Bohemia. Not expecting the soon-to-be Public Enemy Number One, the owner opened the door to the three men. They yanked the telephone from the wall and demanded a car. There were a few guests, and the owner's wife was ill and laying on a couch. "You couldn't be Dillinger, could you?" the woman asked. In the midst of the chaos, Dillinger immediately turned charming. Grinning as he placed a blanket over her he said, "Now, Mother, I'm John Dillinger, but I'm not as bad as they make me out." The owner later commented, "For an outlaw, that Dillinger was a gentleman. He made the others behave. There was no foul language."

But Dillinger was not at this resort for a social call. He discovered that a hired hand had a Model-A Ford and forced him to get dressed and prepare the car for a getaway. For some reason, before they drove away, Dillinger demanded that everyone in the resort stand on the porch. Even the ill woman was made to join the group. But Dillinger, ever gallant, again wrapped a blanket around the woman. With the hired hand at the wheel (he would be dumped out several

Although Dillinger and his gang did not leave behind many personal items authorities could use to track them down, they did abandon a cache of weapons, including pistols and Thompson submachine guns.

miles down the road and given seven dollars), Dillinger, Hamilton, and Van Meter drove off into the night toward Saint Paul.

Back at Little Bohemia, the federal agents were guarding a building that no longer held any of the gang members. When daylight arrived it was decided to begin a raid with tear gas. To add insult to injury (two men had been killed already) the tear-gas cylinders hit the window screens of the lodge, bounced onto the ground, and sent fumes back toward the lawmen. When agents began shooting, three women came out of the basement with their hands in the air. One was Nelson's wife, Helen. The agents continued firing on the lodge. The Wanatkas watched as their home and business were blasted with bullets. Purvis finally realized that the outlaws were long gone.

While Dillinger had not been captured, what he left behind was of interest to the law enforcement officials. Sometimes the possessions provided clues, other times they did not. This time there was little left to offer any clues. Dillinger left only a tin of aspirins, chocolate Ex-Lax, tooth powder, shaving cream, and bandages. There was also a large leather satchel, but if it had contained money the cash was gone with its owner.

Although tragic due to the loss of life, Will Rogers again found humor in the episode in the Wisconsin woods. "Well, they had Dillinger surrounded and was all ready to shoot him when he come out," wrote Rogers, "but another bunch of folks come out ahead, so they just shot them instead. Dillinger is going to accidently get with some innocent bystanders some time, and then he will get shot." Others also found Dillinger's escapes comical. A street vendor is reported to have sold envelopes for fifty cents saying there was a photo of Dillinger inside. When a person bought the envelope and opened it they found it empty. "See," said the vendor, "he got away from you too."

In spite of his uncanny ability to escape, Dillinger was not yet safe. The three bandits were chased briefly to Ladysmith, Wisconsin, by a county sheriff before crossing the Mississippi River at Red Wing, Minnesota. Heading north, they were again accosted by a county sheriff, this one from Minnesota. The gang's slow Model A was being pursued by a sheriff's car equally short on horsepower. Bullets began to be exchanged and Hamilton, who some thought a "bullet magnet" due to his many wounds, was shot while riding in the car's backseat. This led Dillinger to return fire and a fifty-mile chase began through the suburbs of Minneapolis and Saint Paul. Without two-way radios the lawmen finally lost the old car carrying the crooks two miles from where the chase had begun.

Realizing they needed faster transportation, Dillinger and Van Meter hijacked a family driving a Ford V-8. They placed Hamilton, bleeding badly from his back wounds, in the backseat. They ordered the husband, wife, and little boy to get back into their car with the gang. The woman recognized Dillinger. Noting her fear he said, "Don't worry about the kid. We like kids." He even bought the boy a bottle of soda when they stopped for gas. The gang dropped the family off in the country and finding Saint Paul too hot for comfort, headed the speedy stolen Ford toward Chicago. A Milwaukee, Wisconsin, dealership produced a brochure that asked the question, "Will they catch John Dillinger?" to which it answered "Not until they get him out of a Ford V-8."

Chicago police put out a call for the Ford V-8 but again, with few two-way radios to receive the bulletin, Dillinger and Van Meter made it safely back to Chicago. Hamilton's wound proved fatal and he died a week later on April 26. Dillinger and the others buried him outside Chicago and covered his body with lye to disfigure his features in case he was found. Dillinger was supposed to have said to Hamilton's corpse, "I know you'd do as much for me."

Reilly and his wounded girlfriend did make it to Saint Paul, as did Carroll. Nelson, after killing the federal agent, had driven in circles before miring his car in mud only twelve miles from Little Bohemia. Lost, he walked eighteen miles to an Indian reservation, where he hid out for several days with a Native American named Ollie Catfish. After stealing, buying, and wrecking two or three more cars, Nelson safely made it back to Chicago. In less than two weeks the ever-active Nelson was back in Indiana, where he beat up two policemen and chased two others away after shooting up their squad car.

Dillinger had miraculously escaped again. Local and state officials had been made to look ridiculous by the Hoosier outlaw. The most obvious example had been the repeated failures of Leach. Dillinger had now made Hoover and his men look equally silly. The Bureau agents had botched an almost guaranteed capture in Saint Paul and also at Dillinger's father's farm in Indiana. Now the major failure in Wisconsin was again by Hoover's men. (So sure was he of success, Hoover had unwisely announced to the press in the middle of the night that Dillinger was surrounded.) The Bureau continued to look ridiculous in the raid's aftermath when it offered the Wanatkas only thirty dollars to repair their heavily damaged lodge. In addition, the dealership that had rented the automobiles to the agents had to sue the federal government for its money.

A childhood friend of Wanatka's son visited the lodge three days after the raid. The smell of tear gas still filled the rooms and the place was shot to pieces. "It was a real mess," the man recalled years later. One obvious lesson from the fiasco at Little Bohemia was that the Bureau should have worked with local authorities who knew the territory. One or two well-placed roadblocks might have captured Dillinger and his gang.

The outraged citizens of northern Wisconsin circulated a petition calling for Purvis to be fired. The petition pointed to the "irresponsible conduct of federal operatives" for having raided Little Bohemia "in such a stupid manner as to bring about the deaths of two men and injury to four others." They noted none of the dead or injured were the crooks being pursued. Purvis did offer his resignation, but Hoover refused to accept it. He supported both Purvis and Clegg and said very little else about the fiasco. He had, after all, hired these men and been giving them directions every day. Purvis's son, Alston, admitted that the Little Bohemia raid was a disaster and did not help the agency's reputation. But Alston did defend his father and the agents. "Mistakes were made," he said. "But the most distinguishing feature of the raid was the bravery and dedication of those seventeen agents."

Newspaper cartoons ridiculed Attorney General Homer Cummings, making Dillinger out to be the smarter of the two men. After Little Bohemia, an official in the Justice Department in Washington declared, "I don't know where or when we get him [Dillinger], but we will get him. And you can say for me that I hope we will get him under such circumstances that the government won't have to stand the expense of a trial." This very much seemed like a shoot-to-kill order which others, including Hoover, later refuted. Cummings, Hoover's boss, seemed to reverse the director's more limited orders by stating the policy would be "Shoot to kill—

Between 1933 and 1944, President Franklin D. Roosevelt gave thirty evening radio addresses on a number of issues that became known as "fireside chats." The term came from Harry C. Butcher of the CBS network.

then count to ten."

Immediately after "The Battle of Little Bohemia," as some in the press referred to it, Purvis was probably at the lowest point in his career. One Wisconsin newspaper referred to the lawmen as "Comic Opera Cops." The *Chicago Times* saw no humor when two men were killed and the bad guys got away. Purvis countered that the Bureau had gained important evidence in the raid, but not much. He did find out for the first time that Dillinger and Nelson had been working together. More than a dozen pieces of luggage divulged nothing but guns, license plates, and clothes. Oddly there was even an overdue book from a Minnesota library.

The federal government was getting tired of Dillinger and the circuses that seemed to occur whenever his capture was attempted. When the dust had settled it was not only Purvis's job that was on the line. The Little Bohemia affair had put Hoover in a difficult situation with his superiors. More than one politician in Washington thought Hoover himself should be fired or demoted. Congress estimated that in one year all murders, kidnappings, and robberies had cost the country $15 million.

After the failure at Little Bohemia, Dillinger regained the attention of the U.S. president. The *Tulsa Daily World*, for example, had the headline "Roosevelt Roused by Dillinger." In a fireside chat a week after Little Bohemia, Roosevelt again pushed for his crime bill. He also scolded those in the public who tolerated criminals and corrupt officials or "applauded and romanticized crime." Roosevelt, still in the first year of his New Deal program, looked to federal rather than local authorities to solve the nation's crime problems. Page one of the *New York Times* on April 24, 1934 read, "New Dillinger Killings Stir the President—Asks for Quick Crime Bills."

When the crime bill was signed on May 18, Roosevelt said that his New Deal was going to "curb the evil-doer" whoever it might be. The legislation gave the Bureau two hundred more agents. Cummings also requested armored cars and airplanes to catch the outlaws.

The government was concerned because the public was concerned. The Associated Press estimated (the estimate may or may not have had any basis in fact) that the government had spent $2 million chasing Dillinger when he had stolen less than a quarter of that amount. While the Little Bohemia escape was the big news story, the press also brought it to the nation's attention that Dillinger had made an additional escape that night while in Saint Paul. April had again been a month where Dillinger eluded a multitude of lawmen, adding to the outlaw's apparent invincibility.

Newspapers and magazines believed that the crime problem went deeper than Hoover, Purvis, and the federal government. Prisons, prosecutors, and parole boards all came in for criticism. Weak local police departments and communities (such as Mooresville, Indiana) often protected their hometown hoodlums. Even the "molls" who helped their boyfriends were viewed as part of the problem. There were also calls by the Roosevelt administration for stricter gun regulations. This included serial numbers, gun permits, and character references to own any kind of firearm. Gun manufacturers and hunters put up little resistance to these ideas.

In his book *Dillinger's Wild Ride*, Elliot Gorn wrote, "John Dillinger had become something quite extraordinary. He had become somebody. He was famous." Gorn added that the common people of the Great Depression had mixed feelings about the gentleman bandit. People felt a rage toward an economic system that was failing and hurting them. Yet, what Dillinger was doing was both inspiring and fascinating to many. When shown in newsreels at movie theaters he was often cheered. But parents clearly did not want their children to follow the outlaw's example.

For all the incredible getaways and the seemingly positive outlook the public held about him, the truth was that Dillinger's life was not getting any easier. Upon recovering several of the getaway cars from the night at Little Bohemia, Purvis stated that Dillinger was dead. This was based on the amount of blood found in the two abandoned Fords. But the blood was Hamilton's, who was now dead. Dillinger was angry over what had happened in Wisconsin and upset about rumors that he had not really escaped the Crown Point jail on his own. He told friends that he would never be taken alive—in fact, he welcomed a shootout with police. This reckless talk from Dillinger was unusual. On the move in Chicago and northern Indiana, Dillinger planned his next project. Although shorthanded, the duo of Dillinger and Van Meter decided it was time to hit another bank.

9

Hiding in Plain Sight

Although not seen since the Little Bohemia raid in mid-April, by early May of 1934 John Dillinger was still on the minds of most Americans. On May 7 *Time* magazine published a four-page feature titled "Bad Man at Large." Within the piece was a "game" called "Dillinger Land." Dotted lines drawn in loops and circles covered the "board," which was a map of the Midwest. Skull and crossbones identified the places where deaths had occurred. There was not room on the map for all the robberies. In addition there were marks on the map showing where Dillinger had stopped for gasoline and even had his hair cut. Photographs and brief biographies of the gang accompanied the article. *Time's* competitor, *Newsweek*, actually ran more stories on the outlaw. But what was going on was neither a game nor a journalistic rivalry.

The stakes in this chase were high. "Looks like if the Democrats don't get Dillinger they may lose this fall's election," quipped Will Rogers. A cartoon in *Collier's* magazine (June 2, 1934) showed Dillinger surprising two inept guards labeled "Law Enforcement" and "Politics." The magazine went on to make the point that federal resources were needed to handle cases too difficult for local sheriffs. The Democrats and President Franklin D. Roosevelt, however, did not sit idly by. They passed additional anticrime legislation and appealed to the public to help authorities. Thirty-eight of J. Edgar Hoover's Bureau of Investigation agents were reportedly assigned solely to Dillinger.

Years later Alston Purvis, Melvin Purvis's son, may have said it best when describing Dillinger's mode of operation: "It was [his] genius to rob a bank in one state, flee into another, and sleep in a third, thus confounding local police and giving the impression that he could be literally anywhere. Dillinger was a phantom . . . zigzagging across the heartland in a dizzying display of criminal [self-confidence.]" Tales of Dillinger being right under the noses of the police are many. He is reported to have more than once stopped a policeman to ask if he had seen John Dillinger. Homer Van Meter and Dillinger also impersonated officials of the New Deal's National Recovery Act, going into banks and asking questions about security. A Baltimore newspaper wondered how such ineptness could happen. They noted that Dillinger's picture was in every police station and post office in the nation and yet no one could find him—until he robbed a bank.

How Dillinger selected the banks he robbed followed no pattern. Sometimes he struck banks based on tips from fellow crooks. Others were due to their location or may have been "inside jobs." On May 3, 1934, Fostoria, Ohio, was the next target and Dillinger could have thrown a dart at a map to select it. Fostoria was located in northeastern Ohio with a population of less than 10,000. Dillinger and Van Meter walked into the lobby of the bank through an attached drugstore. Tommy Carroll served as the getaway driver. Dillinger and Van Meter each pulled Thompson machine guns from beneath their coats and gave the command, "Stick 'em up."

Some experts do not credit Dillinger for the Fostoria job, but they are probably wrong. A license plate connected Dillinger to the robbery and a number of eyewitnesses claimed it was him. Bank jobs were not getting any easier to carry off, as this one proved. Van Meter, taking on the role of the absent Baby Face Nelson, seemed extremely trigger happy. He fired shots at or near various employees, no doubt to intimidate them. The glass separating the lobby from the bank cages and counters was shattered by submachine-gun blasts. For good measure and no doubt effect, Van Meter blew the head of a mounted stuffed elk off the wall.

The town's police chief, on the scene almost immediately, was just as quickly shot in the chest by Van Meter. A misfired shot from the wounded police chief then hit a bank employee. Outside, Carroll randomly began spraying bullets up and down the street. While their cash take was a disappointing $15,000, other reports indicate a larger sum in bonds. Police, arriving on the scene almost as fast as their chief, had held their fire for fear of hitting the parade of robbers and hostages coming out of the bank. Still, four citizens were shot in the scuffle as the group made their way to the getaway car.

Dillinger was thought not to be part of the Fostoria heist due to his low profile during the robbery. But Van Meter had been directed by Dillinger to take the lead while he served in a backup role. It has been speculated that authorities may have downplayed or ignored the robbery to give less importance to Dillinger's growing fame. He was also blamed for robberies in Flint, Michigan, and Chicago that were clearly not his. But there is little doubt it was indeed Dillinger in Fostoria on that spring day.

Two weeks later, on May 21, Dillinger and Van Meter hit another bank in north-central Ohio, this one in Galion, but only came away with about $5,000. Dillinger was easily identified as he bounded over the cashier's cage. The reason for the small take was that Dillinger no longer took his usual time during a robbery. If it looked as though accessing the safe was going to take too much time, he left. In addition, banks were hiring more guards, who increasingly were able to match the crooks' firepower. Only a few shots were fired in Galion before the pair made their getaway. It was also noted that the "Gentleman Johnnie" of previous robberies, full of smiles and wisecracks, was gone. Now it was all business.

Between the two Ohio robberies, on May 10, Dillinger slipped into Indianapolis to drop off money at his half brother's gasoline station. Not overly generous considering he had just taken several thousand in the Fostoria robbery, he told his nephew to give five hundred dollars to his father and the same amount to his sister. There was a hundred dollars for the nephew and a hundred dollars was to go to his brother-in-law. What was remarkable about this drop-off was that a Bureau agent observed the whole transaction. The Bureau had placed an agent across the street from the gas station on the chance their prey would show up. When Dillinger arrived that day he wore baggy overalls and a blue shirt along with a vest and tie. He also wore a large hat and glasses. The agent at first thought him too large to be the five-foot, seven-inch tall Dillinger. Then he noticed the deep cleft in the unshaven chin. This facial marking made Dillinger easy to identify and the agent decided to follow. He was within a hundred feet of him when Dillinger turned the corner onto Washington Street and vanished into thin air. He was gone again.

While out of sight, Dillinger was never far out of mind—especially the mind of the public. Students in Ohio put on a school play about him, while children in Wisconsin dressed up like his gang for a town parade. When Mr. William Van Til, a teacher in Columbus, Ohio, asked his high school boys what they wanted to study, he was told "crooks." An abandoned car Dillinger had used was in a traveling carnival show. The idea he was not such a bad fellow again emerged. Some citizens called for "Christian forgiveness" or to just let him alone. The bankers continued to be blamed for their greedy practices and the idea that Dillinger would make a wonderful policeman was also suggested.

Most of the month of May Dillinger had been in Chicago and northwest Indiana. The two matters most on his mind were Billie Frechette's trial in Minnesota and having a facelift or what was becoming known as plastic surgery. These may have been the reasons behind Dillinger's thriftiness with his family. Paying his lawyer Louis Piquett to represent Frechette and finding a surgeon for the operation on his face were both expensive. Keeping out of sight was becoming more and more difficult unless he left the country—his face was just too well-known for him to walk down any street in America. Governors of five midwestern states had pooled their resources into a reward fund. Not trusting anyone to find them a hideout, Dillinger and Van Meter decided to live in a paneled delivery truck.

The red Ford truck held two makeshift beds and they amazingly stayed briefly in a tourist park in Crown Point, Indiana. When later asked if he was afraid to return to the site of his famous jailbreak Dillinger answered, "Why Crown Point is the safest place in America." It was in fact one of the last places he was being sought. Bureau and state officials were looking elsewhere, asking Canadian and British officials to be on the lookout for Dillinger. Rather than in Europe or north of the border, Dillinger was in the back of the truck ill with a fever and mentally depressed. The pressure on him was taking its toll.

Back in Saint Paul, Minnesota, in late May, Piquett put on an impressive show in the courtroom attempting to free Frechette. The trial had begun in mid-May of 1934. In the case, *U.S. v. Evelyn Frechette*, the court gave nine aliases she had allegedly used. Yet there was little doubt that the trial was more about Dillinger than Frechette. Piquett led the defense, assisted by Jerome Hoffman. The controversial portion of the trial was federal agent Harold Reinecke's testimony about Frechette's treatment while in custody in Chicago. Under stiff cross examination by Hoffman, Reinecke denied that Frechette had been beaten, threatened, or placed under strong lights when questioned. The agent only admitted that he put his fingers "gently" under her chin to get her to look at him. He acknowledged that Frechette was held by federal agents without informing anyone of her location.

Piquett later claimed that during the trial Dillinger pulled up in front of the courthouse in Saint Paul and quietly got the lawyer's attention. "What are you doing here?" asked Piquett. "You're hotter than a firecracker in this town!" After asking how the trial was going, Dillinger assured Piquett he would be paid and drove off saying, "So long, Counsel. See you in Chicago."

Frechette nearly freed herself in Saint Paul. Imitating her boyfriend's talent at escaping, Frechette, during a recess in the trial, almost walked out of the courthouse unnoticed, but was stopped by a police officer at the last minute. Although rarely paid for his services by Dillinger, Piquett put on a splendid performance in his closing argument. "Evelyn Frechette loved Johnnie Dillinger," he declared, "and although she knew he was a desperado, she was willing to take a chance with him. We all know where Dillinger belongs . . . but are we going to punish . . . Miss Frechette who was willing to go to the end with this Public Enemy Number One because she loved him?" Piquett's plea failed, and Frechette was sentenced to two years in jail for harboring her criminal boyfriend.

With Frechette behind bars, Dillinger turned his attention to changing his appearance. Due to the horrendous wounds soldiers experienced during World War I, the art of facial reconstruction had rapidly advanced. While nowhere near the sophistication of modern-day surgeons, plastic surgery in the 1930s was considered a practical, if not perfect option, to change one's looks. Increasingly hunted, Dillinger thought it was one of the few ways to keep alive. On May 23, 1934, he was reminded of the danger when Bonnie Parker and Clyde Barrow were ambushed by lawmen from Texas and Louisiana. They were killed in a hail of bullets on a rural road in Bienville Parish, Louisiana. Dillinger, however, never considered himself in the same criminal class as the famous Texas couple, who mainly robbed gasoline stations and grocery stores.

Dillinger had actually started thinking about changing his appearance in March or April 1934. He inquired about plastic surgery and asked Piquett and if he knew anyone who could arrange for the procedure. "I'd like to have him [the doctor] work on me," he said. "I want to live like other people. Billie and I would like to be married and settle down somewhere." On other occasions, Dillinger was heard to say, "I'd like to have enough money to enjoy life; be clear of everything—not worry; take care of my old man, and see a ball game every day."

On May 24 two East Chicago policemen attempted to pull Dillinger and Van Meter over in their red panel truck. The

A 1933 photograph of outlaws Clyde Barrow and Bonnie Parker found by police in a hideout in Joplin, Missouri.

policemen had been part of the city's Dillinger Squad since the
January killing of Sergeant William O'Malley. Dillinger later told
an associate of Piquett that Van Meter, using a machine gun, had
killed the two policemen. Dillinger's story was that another East
Chicago policeman, Martin Zarkovich, had sent the two men to
look for Dillinger knowing there was a good chance they would
be shot. Supposedly, Dillinger had been paying off East Chicago
police and someone became too greedy or knew too much. Such a
crooked East Chicago police connection has never been proven. As
he told the story, Dillinger disliked the shooting of the lawmen,
later saying, "Those two police should never have been bumped off.
They were just trying to do their job. They knew too much and Zark
[Zarkovich] was getting antsy. I think Van felt bad about it, but
there was nothing else that he could do."

For Dillinger, changing his appearance was becoming more
urgent every day. Piquett and his associate began working on the
plastic surgery scheme upon returning from Frechette's trial in
Minnesota. First, on May 27, they rented a room from a sleazy
ex-convict named James "Jimmy" Probasco. The cost for housing
Dillinger and Van Meter, who was also considering going under the
knife, would be thirty-five dollars a day. Probasco had first asked
for fifty dollars, but Dillinger balked at the price. "Don't you think
that's high?" asked Dillinger. Probasco replied, "Well, you're pretty
hot you know."

The cost for the procedure on Dillinger's face and to have his
fingerprints removed came to $5,000. A seedy physician with a
criminal record was recruited along with an equally shady doctor
who administered ether (an anesthetic). The plan was to alter
Dillinger's appearance by removing two moles from between his

eyes, a small dent from the bridge of his nose, and a scar on his lip. The famous and highly noticeable cleft or dimple on his chin would be filled in and his cheeks pulled higher, in other words, a facelift.

The surgery took place in Dillinger's hired room on the evening of May 28. The doctor washed his hands and had the outlaw take off his shirt and lay on a cot. When the anesthetic was given to Dillinger by the assisting doctor, something went wrong. The ether was being applied by dripping it through a towel placed over Dillinger's face. Since the ether did not seem to be putting him to sleep, the doctor poured even more onto the cloth. Dillinger started choking, began to swallow his tongue, and passed out. The doctor administering the anesthesia panicked, shouting, "My God, he's dead!" The other physician pulled Dillinger's tongue out of his throat with a pair of surgical clamps. He also gave the outlaw mouth-to-mouth resuscitation and began pumping his arms against his chest to get the heart going again.

Once the doctor switched to a local anesthetic, the operation proved to be long and difficult. Dillinger had lied to the doctor about not having eaten, when in fact he had a large meal an hour before the operation. As a result the patient vomited several times. He also lost a significant amount of blood. The ordeal took seven hours. "You nearly died on us," he was told after the operation. "It might just as well have been now as some other time," Dillinger laughed.

The assisting physician stayed five days with Dillinger at Probasco's house. On June 2 Dillinger, not pleased with the surgery's outcome, sent word that he wanted more work done. Even after his partner's unhappy experience, Van Meter decided he also wanted to change his looks. The next day the physician returned to remove the men's fingerprints with hydrochloric acid and do more surgery on Dillinger's face. The dimple in his chin was the problem and it needed additional attention. Worried about his close call with ether, Dillinger had the procedure done while awake. Van Meter also went under the knife that day.

At first Dillinger was unhappy with the surgery, saying he appeared to have "snorted wildcats" up his nose and did not look any different than before the surgery. He later calmed down and seemed fairly pleased with the results. An angry Van Meter was not and threatened to shoot the doctor. He thought that he looked like he had been in a dogfight. "What a mess they made out of me!" he yelled. "I paid out five thousand dollars and what did I get for it?" Van Meter's features were such that altering his appearance may have been next to impossible. While Dillinger could live with the work he had done, in truth the procedure did little to change his appearance. One report had Nelson present at the Probasco house during this week. If so, he evidently chose to leave his childlike features untouched.

While Dillinger was undergoing surgery, Nelson was having good luck eluding the law. Believing the devoted husband would try to contact or visit his wife, Helen, the Bureau staked out her apartment in Chicago. They also hired a gas-station attendant across the street to call if he saw Nelson, who arrived one day, drove around the block five times, and, seeing no agents, went inside for a visit. The attendant later admitted that he recognized Nelson, but did not call anyone. "Why?" he was asked. "No one gave me a phone number," he replied.

Back in Washington, Hoover decided that the Bureau was staffed with too many lawyers and accountants. Early in May he began bringing in firearm experts from Texas, including a man named Charles Winstead. These men would train Hoover's agents and also be ready to assist if and when Dillinger was located. There is little doubt about the true purpose of these men being hired. Bringing in high-powered, experienced lawmen meant the idea of capturing Dillinger alive might have changed to shooting him. He had gotten away too many times for Hoover. Bad tips on Dillinger's whereabouts had Purvis running all over Indiana, which did not help. Purvis was demoted and one of Hoover's top aids, Sam Cowley, was dispatched to Chicago to take over the Dillinger case.

As Hoover was making his moves, members of the Dillinger gang continued to meet with bad ends. His part-time getaway driver, Carroll, was gunned down in Waterloo, Iowa. A gas-station attendant saw guns in his car and called the police. When the police arrived Carroll pulled a gun and then ran. He was killed with four shots to the back. Carroll's girlfriend was grilled by the police, but she knew nothing of Dillinger's whereabouts. It was reported that an angry Nelson showed up in Waterloo looking for the man who "turned a nickel" (the cost of a telephone call in 1934) on his buddy. The man had wisely left town.

May had turned to June and Dillinger was getting impatient to hit the streets again. Three days after the final "touch ups" to his face, he believed he was ready to rejoin society. Dillinger was first seen in Chicago by fellow criminals in a tavern on June 5. His face had a puffy and wider look than before the operation. The identifiable features—the moles and dimple in his chin—were gone. The crooked smile remained, but a darker hair-dye job and the addition of a mustache and eyeglasses gave Dillinger a new confidence that he was unrecognizable.

There is debate over how successful the plastic surgery was

for Dillinger. Some who knew him well saw no difference in his appearance and wondered why he was spending so much time in public. He repeatedly went to Chicago Cubs baseball games and often ran into Piquett, who was not impressed with his client's new face and told Dillinger it would be wise to leave Wrigley Field, which he did. On June 8 Dillinger was again at Wrigley Field and ran into Piquett. Just then Captain Stege of the Chicago Dillinger Squad appeared. "Fuzz [police]," Piquett whispered to his client, "Big fuzz." Dillinger left the ballpark in a hurry.

The visits to Wrigley Field continued, Piquett later said. One day, Chicago detectives offhandedly asked Piquett at the ballpark when his client planned to surrender. The lawyer lied, saying he had not seen him for weeks. According to Piquett, Dillinger had been sitting twenty feet away during the entire conversation. Another Chicago Cubs story has a Crown Point, Indiana, man speaking to someone he thought was Dillinger. By the time the man retrieved several policemen, Dillinger was gone. For the last several weeks of his life then, Dillinger hid in plain sight.

A view of Wrigley Field from the centerfield bleachers, circa 1930.

On June 9 Dillinger and Van Meter went to Indianapolis, possibly to kill Art McGinnis, an informant for Matt Leach and others. McGinnis was spotted by the two men, but made a getaway. This story may or may not be accurate, but at times Dillinger did have outbursts where he seemed bent on revenge for being double-crossed. The pair returned to Chicago the same day. On the trip back they had a flat tire and two Indiana State Policemen stopped to help. Van Meter pointed a machine gun at them and they left.

Dillinger also made strong threats against Reinecke. His fellow

A portrait of Rita "Polly" Hamilton found in Dillinger's watch after his death.

gang members stopped him from going after the Bureau agent.
Dillinger was alleged to have wanted to kill Purvis, but his Chicago
lawyer said the federal agent was only doing his job. The outlaw
decided to leave Purvis alone, but still wanted to go after Reinecke.
He never did. Piquett was quite direct with Dillinger about such
would-be killings and said if he pulled one, "I'm not with you any
longer, Johnnie." Dillinger calmed down and decided to "let it ride
for the time being."

Frechette, according to those who knew Dillinger well, was the
love of his life. But she was in jail. Dillinger lost little time finding a
new girlfriend. On Monday, June 11, he met Rita "Polly" Hamilton.
Similar in looks to Frechette, Hamilton was a part-time waitress
and part-time prostitute. From North Dakota and, like Frechette, of
Native American heritage, she was twenty-six years old, stood five
feet, three and had blue eyes and red hair. The couple met through
Anna Sage, a Romanian living in northeast Indiana and Chicago.
Dillinger and Hamilton spent the next seven weeks together.
Around July 4 Dillinger moved into Sage's apartment in Chicago.
Dillinger told Hamilton that his name was Jimmy Lawrence and
that he worked downtown at the Chicago Board of Trade. He left
on occasional "business trips," but mainly stayed in the city. When
Hamilton asked about the scars on his face, Dillinger told her that
he had been in a recent automobile accident. She believed him.

After Dillinger's death Hamilton provided considerable detail
about "Jimmy Lawrence." Her comments make it clear that Dillinger
impressed her. His behavior around her may have been authentic
or merely a front to keep her in the dark about his true identity. "I
was crazy about him," she said. Hamilton thought him intelligent
and fascinating. Polly found Dillinger was solidly built, displayed

an engaging smile, and spoke with a low, pleasant voice. He was a "good dresser, clean and neat." In addition he was an excellent card player (usually pinochle and rummy) and not a bad singer. Most important to a young woman during the Great Depression, "Jimmy" liked to go out in the evenings. He paid for Hamilton to get her teeth fixed and bought her gifts. He loved movies and amusement parks, did not drink much or use rough language. After meals he even washed the dishes. "He really couldn't have been kind and good and do the things he did," Hamilton concluded.

Dillinger may have been seeing Sage before he took up with Hamilton. He seemed confident around her due to his new appearance. Staying late one evening in a restaurant with Sage, Dillinger observed the owner emptying his cash box and counting the money in front of him. Looking at the owner, he said with his crooked grin, "Aren't you afraid John Dillinger might drop in and take it away from you?" The owner turned and said, "No, he just robs from the crooked banks. If he knew I needed money he'd probably give it to me." Gratified by the man's remark, Dillinger replied as he left, "Yeah, he probably would."

A number of questions remain unanswered about Dillinger. One of the major unknowns about the last year of his life was the connection between him and the East Chicago police. Some have maintained that protection money may have changed hands with lawmen in northwest Indiana. Others speculate this may have led to his demise. Sage's former boyfriend was Zarkovich, the East Chicago policeman possibly involved earlier in the alleged double police murder by Van Meter. He had a past, having been convicted, and then let go on appeal, for taking bribes. Zarkovich may have known much about Dillinger's location and movements. Having his friend Sage set Dillinger up with a Frechette "look-alike" might not have been a coincidence. The East Chicago police connection may also have played a part in the outlaw's Crown Point jailbreak. It is fairly certain that Sage knew Hamilton's boyfriend was Dillinger, not Jimmy Lawrence. Dillinger had a sixth sense for danger, but for some reason he trusted Sage. It proved to be a fatal mistake.

Sage's son, Steve, said that Dillinger "never flashed a roll [money] on me. I never saw any great amount of money on him. If he was the man they said he was, he was an all-around fellow. He didn't act tough and he didn't talk rough." Dary Matera in his book *John Dillinger: The Life and Death of America's First Celebrity Criminal* suggests that Dillinger was actually playing against type, almost acting the role of a "sissy." He seemed mild-mannered, not the least bit threatening. Even with the stylish clothes and the easygoing behavior, some saw beneath the disguise. Hamilton's waitress friends noted that her new boyfriend sure looked a lot like Dillinger.

In the 2009 film *Public Enemies*, actor Johnny Depp, portraying Dillinger, replicated an incredible piece of real-life nerve and daring. Dillinger accompanied Hamilton to the Chicago Police Building, where she was applying for a waitress permit. Hamilton conducted her business only two floors from the offices of the group devoted to finding her new boyfriend. Dillinger seems to have loitered in the lobby, walking right by policemen assigned to find him, and even visited a squad room. He apparently did this four times—three times in June and once in July. No one ever reported seeing him in the building.

If Dillinger was not noticed by the authorities it was not for lack of opportunities. Hamilton later claimed that Dillinger walked close to police in public places, showing little concern that he would be spotted. "That must have been why it took them so long to catch him," she said. "He was always right under their noses where they weren't looking for him."

Central Indiana seemed to draw Dillinger back again and again. He did not, however, visit his family's Mooresville farm or his sister. His father placed a letter in an Indianapolis newspaper on June 16 specifically stating that his son had not been in Mooresville on April 22 and April 28. Why he selected those dates is not known. Dillinger had been at the farm in early April. Somewhere around mid-June Dillinger was in Indianapolis. He paid a visit to Indianapolis newspaper reporter, Tubby Toms, who had received Dillinger's lucky rabbit foot while in Tucson, Arizona. Pulling up in a new Hudson Terraplane to the reporter's home, Dillinger said, "Get in. I want to talk with you a minute."

Toms was not sure of the visit's exact purpose. It seemed Dillinger wanted to set the record straight about bank jobs he had been falsely accused of doing. He told the reporter where he had supposedly been on those days. Mistaken sightings did occur on a regular basis. The items on the outlaw's agenda seemed to be whether a deal might be arranged to give himself up. The reporter thought Dillinger may have wanted a "truce" and pardon from the Indiana governor Paul V. McNutt, whose history with Dillinger made that highly unlikely. Toms made it clear that he would report their meeting to the authorities. This did not seem to bother Dillinger. He did request a half an hour's head start. Exactly thirty minutes later, Toms called Leach. But by that time Dillinger had disappeared.

While pretending to be the "nice guy," underneath Dillinger was all business. Hearing his lawyer had not made payments to men

Dillinger owed money to, he wrote Piquett a stern letter on June 20. In part Dillinger said, "You know I sent you the money to pay everyone that I owe. I'm telling them I have sent you the money. And when they come to you, you can tell them why you did not pay them. So far as I'm concerned, you and I are through." Piquett admitted he had spent the money on himself. "Well, he is right," Piquett said. "I did not do the right thing. I was busted and I owed office rent and office help."

On June 22 Dillinger turned thirty-one years old. This was the day that U.S. Attorney General Homer Cummings officially made him Public Enemy Number One. Chicago police had previously given Dillinger the title. His loving and loyal sister, Audrey, placed this message in the personal columns of an Indianapolis paper: "Birthday greetings to my darling brother, John Dillinger, on his 31st birthday. Wherever he may be, I hope he will read this message. Audrey Hancock." The next day Cummings added an additional $15,000 to the reward on Dillinger's head. On that same day, which was also Polly Hamilton's birthday, she and Dillinger celebrated for two days in the Chicago Loop district. The outlaw became more and more bold appearing in public. Although his barber called the police twice on Dillinger, they never followed up.

A major hurdle in capturing Dillinger was finding out where he was hiding—nobody was really sure. This led to sightings of him that became comical, even ridiculous, at times. He was reported to have dressed like woman, a nun, a Native American, and also an African American. In early summer he was sighted in cities across the United States. The pursuits were also embarrassing. At one point, police from Illinois and Indiana were chasing each other on the streets of Chicago, each thinking Dillinger was in the other's car.

WANTED

JOHN HERBERT DILLINGER

On June 23, 1934, HOMER S. CUMMINGS, Attorney General of the United States, under the
authority vested in him by an Act of Congress approved June 6, 1934, offered a reward of

$10,000.00

for the capture of John Herbert Dillinger or a reward of

$5,000.00

for information leading to the arrest of John Herbert Dillinger.

DESCRIPTION

Age, 32 years; Height, 5 feet 7-1/8 inches;
Weight, 153 pounds; Build, medium; Hair,
medium chestnut; Eyes, grey; Complexion,
medium; Occupation, machinist; Marks and
scars, 1/2 inch scar back left hand, scar
middle upper lip, brown mole between eyebrows.

    All claims to any of the aforesaid rewards and all questions and disputes that may
arise as among claimants to the foregoing rewards shall be passed upon by the Attorney
General and his decisions shall be final and conclusive. The right is reserved to divide and allocate portions of any of said rewards as between several claimants. No
part of the aforesaid rewards shall be paid to any official or employee of the Depart-

*A Justice Department wanted poster for Dillinger issued in June 1934,
offering a $10,000 award for his capture.*

What exactly were Dillinger's plans in June 1934? He always knew he was in a dangerous and violent business. There was the conversation he had with his father in early April about what to do if the worst occurred. But for all of the chances he seemed to be taking in Chicago and around the Midwest, he did not seem to have a "death wish." Every day he had to be careful, be on the lookout, and be ready for anything that might happen. There was serious talk of giving himself up through his lawyer, Piquett. Others believed that he thought of going to Mexico or even farther south into Latin America. He had also talked to both Frechette and Hamilton about settling down and having a family.

The better known he became, the fewer bank jobs Dillinger seemed to pull. He still had expenses and a commitment to help Pierpont and the others in prison in Ohio. The money went quickly. Being a bank robber became, in a way, an industry—a much bigger operation than just robbing banks. Guns not stolen had to be purchased, as well as cars. Gang members needed multiple hideouts and sometimes medical care. Money and bonds had to be laundered. The prices Dillinger and his friends paid for everything from vehicles to groceries were high. People took advantage, as well as a risk, when dealing with them. Often there was little left after all the expenses were paid.

Nevertheless it appeared he knew of only one to way to make a living, and that meant robbing another bank. It would be his last. The target this time was back in Indiana, in the fairly large city of South Bend in the northern part of the state. The robbery was one of the most controversial, due to questions about who took part in it and exactly how many were in on the robbery—five, maybe six. But many facts about the robbery are known, including that a great deal of planning had gone into this particular job.

It was the last day of June in 1934. Downtown South Bend was busy as usual on this summer morning. A car carrying at least five men pulled up near the Merchant's National Bank on Michigan Street. It is confirmed that Dillinger was with his usual conspirator, Van Meter, and also Nelson. The other two men have never been identified with any certainty. It was 11:00 a.m. when the robbery began.

A man carrying a payroll of several thousand dollars entered the bank guarded by two detectives. Before the delivery was completed, the two policemen surprisingly left for lunch. Four men got out of the Hudson Terraplane, including Dillinger. When a citizen on the sidewalk looked at him, Dillinger displayed a pistol and told him to "scram." Meanwhile, outside, Nelson chased the same man away from the getaway car.

After seeing the suspicious men get out of the car a young man passing by ran across the street to phone the police. As Nelson protected the car, Van Meter stood watch over the front door. Then, with one or two of the unknown accomplices, Dillinger walked into the bank, pulled out his Thompson submachine gun, and yelled, "This is a holdup!" There was little doubt that it was Dillinger. The surgery that made him so confident for the past month evidently had not worked. He was recognized. The bank was crowded, but as author Dary Matera has cleverly written, "Dillinger wasn't planning on standing in line . . . and the bigger the audience, the better the show." Dillinger was bellowing orders to those inside the bank. The South Bend Police Department, whose squad cars did have two-way radios, realized immediately what was taking place on Michigan Street.

Because of the large crowd, a number of customers evidently did not hear Dillinger's command and went about their business.

To get their attention Dillinger took his Thompson machine gun, raised it in the air, and imitating Nelson even down to the smile, shot a round into the ceiling. The noise was deafening and plaster dust filled the room. He now had their undivided attention, if not cooperation. A number of men and women dived under desks, ran to the back of the lobby, and some even crowded into the bank's bathroom. Again, stories differ as to Dillinger's behavior. Some say he was quite serious, while other witnesses say that he gave an impressive performance. Grinning, he seemed to be enjoying the chaos he was causing. The other two inside men were emptying the cash drawers from the tellers' cages into pillowcases.

A policeman arrived, but had no idea what he was walking into. Hearing Dillinger's gunshots, the officer ran toward the bank only to be shot dead, probably by either Nelson or Van Meter. This caused an all-out panic on the streets of South Bend. Just then, several other policemen arrived, but the two outside bandits kept them pinned down behind cars and in stores. Both Nelson and Van Meter reloaded their guns in order to continue the fight. Now the citizens of South Bend decided to enter the fray. This seemed typical, as townspeople felt compelled to become involved during bank robberies. And more and more of them were carrying guns. In a previous robbery it had been citizens who had wounded Dillinger and John Hamilton, not the police.

Nelson became the first to fall prey to the irritated South Bend residents. A jeweler stepped outside his store, aimed his gun, and hit Nelson in the back. The gang was wearing bulletproof vests that covered both sides of their torsos. While the shot did not penetrate the metal vest, it did cause a sharp sting. Nelson turned and saw the jeweler still standing with the gun pointed at him. He spewed bullets from his Thompson at the man, missed him, but did cause extensive damage to nearby automobiles and storefronts. Glass flew everywhere. Nelson did hit an unfortunate bystander in the hip and stomach, seriously wounding him. Van Meter, seeing what was happening, grabbed a half-dozen hostages for cover. He then started walking toward the action, all the while shooting from inside his human shield. Nelson also decided to grab a hostage for protection.

If film clips from the various Dillinger robberies had been gathered and edited into one movie, it would have looked very much like this South Bend robbery. A sixteen-year-old kid who had been watching the events outside the bank decided to charge Nelson from behind, jumping on his back and yelling for someone to shoot the outlaw. He was no match for Nelson, who hit the teenager in the head, threw him through a storefront window, and then shot him. The bullet went through the young man's hand and he wisely played dead among the broken glass. Toying with the unpredictable Nelson was never a good idea.

Back inside the bank Dillinger and the other two men had three pillowcases full of money. They, too, grabbed hostages and headed outside, where they joined Nelson and Van Meter. Although the robbers were surrounded by hostages, the police decided to try to hit one or more of them. One of the inside men was shot by the police, but kept moving toward the getaway car. Two of the hostages were struck by the police, both in the leg. One of them was the bank president. Disregarding the chaos around him, Dillinger kept the group moving toward the car.

Then a bullet hit Van Meter, creasing his forehead. Van Meter, according to witnesses, had taken several bullets. Never one to leave a buddy behind, Dillinger dragged the bleeding Van Meter to the car. Nelson was picked up, and with several hostages still inside and outside the car, the gang headed out of town. Regardless of hostages, bullets continued to fly from citizens and police on one side and the bank robbers on the other. Dillinger had Nelson take the wheel and the "Dillinger Luck" held. A bullet passed through Nelson's hat. If the taller Dillinger had been driving, he surely would have been killed. The gang made their getaway in spite of their car repeatedly being hit. But the battle between the gang and the citizens of South Bend was far from over.

Several police cars and a motorcycle cop pursued the robbers. But the speedy Terraplane proved much too fast for them. In addition, the police encountered roofing nails before their engine blew up. Had they caught up with the gang the posse would have been overwhelmingly outgunned. The robbers did experience a flat tire, but put the spare on in record time and were off again. Back in South Bend the wounded were being treated. Six had been shot and Howard Wagner, a police officer who had been scheduled to retire the next day, had been killed. The gunfire may have been the heaviest of any Dillinger robbery. An airplane was sent up, but Dillinger and his men had hidden an automobile and split up once they recovered it.

Early accounts of Dillinger's exploits did not refer to this robbery as being his work. Some positively identified him, but others were not so sure. Leach arrived in South Bend and announced it was not Dillinger—there was too much gunplay and the witnesses could not agree. Leach, however, was wrong. There is little doubt it was Dillinger, who later said, "The streets were full of police and slugs were flying everywhere. It was a regular battle. I don't know what the people in town thought." Two of the gang had been hit and needed medical attention, so they retreated as usual to Chicago. After everyone was patched up, the take was discovered to be a little less than $30,000—not a great amount considering the dead policeman, the wounded, and all the havoc they had caused. Robbing banks, or as some referred to them, "armed withdrawals," was indeed becoming an increasingly difficult task.

Since the heist took place in Indiana, McNutt again raised the issue of Dillinger's harsh punishment as a youth. A county judge, claimed McNutt, not the governor's parole, was behind all the trouble Dillinger had caused. The statement seemed like the excuse it was. A spokesman from Indiana at a police conference in Chicago agreed: "There does not seem to be an escape from the fact that the state of Indiana made John Dillinger the Public Enemy Number One he is today. There is no doubt in my mind that Johnnie Dillinger's life would have been entirely different had the administration of justice in his case and in the case of his partner [in Mooresville] been comparable considering their previous records." Public officials seemed to be spending more time analyzing why Dillinger robbed banks than in catching him.

While Hoover remained unhappy until he got his man, Purvis believed they were closer to capturing Dillinger. Two Bureau men had been killed, but several molls were in jail and Purvis had received information about Dillinger's new appearance. He did not know exactly what his prey looked like, but knew the moles were gone, the hair was black, and the eyebrows had been narrowed. Purvis also thought that Dillinger was becoming more brazen about appearing in public, which was correct. In addition the federal government had added another $25,000 to the reward already being offered by several states.

While state and federal officials were plotting his capture, Dillinger was making plans of his own. After the South Bend job, Dillinger and Van Meter intended to write a book or make a movie about their adventures. They planned on hiring an experienced writer to help them. Oddly, the men decided on the theme "Crime Does Not Pay." Since they continued to rob banks it was a lesson they themselves had not yet learned. The book or movie, they believed, would be a message to the youth of America. Nothing ever came of the idea.

Dillinger wanted to pull one more big robbery. This time it would be a train, not a bank. The results of the bank jobs, while not small, failed to provide the financial resources needed to leave a life of crime. His vision was a million-dollar haul. "We'll have enough to last us the rest of our lives, and right after it's over we're lamming it out of the country," said Dillinger. There was a story that Dillinger wanted to go to Mexico. It was also rumored he would flee the country, traveling with a family as cover to cross the border. The train robbery and the escape to Mexico were set for late July. But other events that month interfered with Dillinger's plans for the future.

10

The Last Picture Show

As the calendar reached July 1934, John Dillinger pondered that one last big job. With enough money he could escape the country, bringing his pursuit by the law to a halt. The "big job" was going to be a train robbery. Some have suggested that Baby Face Nelson was involved early on in the planning. On the night of July 16, two state policemen happened upon Dillinger, Nelson, his wife, and two other men on a little-used road near Chicago. One of the officers asked the group, "What's the trouble here?" Needing little provocation, Nelson emerged from the dark and fired a volley of bullets at the two troopers. They were hit several times, one badly, but both survived. The gang, which had arrived in three cars, then made a getaway. It was later learned that the group was indeed making plans to rob the Chicago, Milwaukee, Saint Paul and Pacific Railroad mail train.

Dillinger had finally become weary of Nelson and his erratic behavior. He decided the great train robbery would be undertaken as originally planned with a single partner, his trusted pal Homer Van Meter. "We're not cutting anybody else in on this," Dillinger said. "We've got it spotted." The two henchmen had evidently been watching a mail or payroll train that was supposedly carrying millions. All they needed, they claimed, was the "soup," a term for nitroglycerin, a powerful and unstable explosive, to be used to blow the doors off the railroad cars. The next day, Dillinger went to Stevens Point, Wisconsin, scouting for a good place to ambush the train. "Van and I are going to pull off the biggest job of our lives," he is said to have bragged. But the scheming had to be delayed—there was just too much heat on Dillinger.

While Dillinger had visions of blowing up trains and spending the rest of his days in exotic Latin America, at least three plots to capture him were in the works. His plastic surgeon had toyed with the idea of going to the federal agents for the growing reward money. But he lost his nerve and did not follow through. The next plan was connected to Jimmy Probasco, in whose home Dillinger had the surgery and spent time recovering. Some have speculated that the outlaw's lawyer, Louis Piquett, might have been in on this betrayal scheme, as he and Probasco drank together. Dillinger thought this possible threat real enough to call Piquett and ask to meet him the last week of July to talk about surrendering to authorities. The appointment may have been for the purpose of killing Piquett, but that hunch is probably not accurate. Dillinger, with the exception of the aborted attempt to kill Art McGinnis in Indianapolis, never used violence in a premeditated manner.

The third plan under way to capture Dillinger had the best chance for success. The date was Saturday, July 21. On that day Matt Leach of the Indiana State Police was in Culver, Indiana. He had gotten a tip that Dillinger was going to rob a bank there. Leach's information was wrong. But on that same day credible information was working its way to the Bureau of Investigation's Melvin Purvis in Chicago. In spite of the Little Bohemia fiasco, Purvis was still on the Dillinger case. The tip came from Polly

Anna Sage, a brothel madam in Chicago, betrayed Dillinger to the Bureau of Investigation and was with him at the Biograph Theater when he was gunned down by authorities. Sage was later known as the "Lady in Red" for the color of the dress she wore to identify herself to the Bureau's agents.

Hamilton's friend, Anna Sage. Since July 4 the bandit had been living with Hamilton at Sage's apartment on the north side of Chicago. Two East Chicago, Indiana, police—Sage's friend, Martin Zarkovich, and Captain Timothy O'Neil—told Purvis they had solid information on where Dillinger was hiding. The two policemen met that Saturday evening at the Bureau's Chicago headquarters. The two East Chicago cops had approached Chicago's "Dillinger Squad" to discuss working with them. Zarkovich and O'Neil had one condition—they wanted Dillinger killed, not taken alive. The Chicago police, however, had little interest in cooperating with their Indiana counterparts. "I'd even give John Dillinger a chance to surrender," one of the Chicago officers said. While the Chicago lawmen were not interested in this possible lead, Purvis was.

What Zarkovich and O'Neil told Purvis was quite simple— Dillinger was going to attend a movie Sunday night. His contact, he told Purvis, was a woman he knew and this woman had a friend who had been seeing Dillinger. Neither Sage's nor Hamilton's names were given to Purvis. Zarkovich's informant would tell the Bureau in which theater they could find Dillinger. In return for the information, the two policemen wanted the reward money, dropping their demand that Dillinger be killed. Van Meter had always worried about his friend's connection to the East Chicago police and the risks Dillinger was taking. Hamilton and her outlaw boyfriend had been seen all over Chicago during July. Neither did Van Meter like Dillinger's move to the Sage apartment because of the connection the woman had with Zarkovich. "I've no use for the East Chicago bunch," he told Dillinger. "You're going to get yourself killed."

Sage did not tell Zarkovich, or he decided not to tell Purvis, that Dillinger had been living in her apartment since early July.

And while the policemen were after the reward money, there was something of equal importance to Sage. A secret meeting was set between Sage and Purvis for that evening. Getting into Purvis's car and making sure he was a federal agent, Sage made her demand. She was about to be deported to Romania. The deal would be to deliver Dillinger in return for being allowed to stay in the United States. Purvis made no promises to Sage, only saying he would explore what might be done for her. Although this was no guarantee, Sage was so desperate not to be thrown out of the country that she agreed to give the authorities Dillinger.

Purvis and Sage then made plans for Sunday night. Sage was sure that she, Hamilton, and Dillinger would be attending the movies the next evening. She would call Purvis and tell him which Chicago theater they would attend. She thought it would be the Marbro, and Purvis sent agents to check out the theater. Dillinger had evidently not made up his mind which movie he wanted to see. Several Chicago theaters had what was then called "refrigerated air" or air-conditioning. The system was actually large blocks of ice with fans blowing across them. The movies were a welcome escape from the blistering Chicago heat wave that July. On Saturday Dillinger, Hamilton, Sage's son, and two other women had spent the day at the beach on Lake Michigan trying to escape the record-breaking heat. Wearing a new bathing suit and in the company of three women, Dillinger was completely unaware that his capture was being planned.

The eventful day of Sunday, July 22, was hectic and nerve-racking for Purvis. His office was on the nineteenth floor of the Bankers Building in downtown Chicago. Constantly keeping Hoover informed in Washington, D.C., Purvis and his fellow agent Sam

Cowley were busily preparing for that night. Cowley had been brought in by Hoover in June to oversee the Dillinger case, so he technically was Purvis's boss. The word "desperate" has been used when describing how badly Hoover wanted to get Dillinger. He believed his agency's future prestige rode on the successful outcome of this particular hunt. Debates took place about how many men to use, how much involvement to allow on the part of the East Chicago policemen, and also whether to inform local law officials about what was going to occur on their home turf. The decision was to let the East Chicago authorities in, but leave the Chicago police out. There was no stakeout of Sage's apartment, as no one had been told that was where Dillinger lived.

Dillinger played cards most of that Sunday afternoon in the apartment and late in the afternoon Sage prepared fried chicken for dinner. Sages's son and his girlfriend had left the apartment. Time was growing short for Purvis and Cowley to get their agents in place. They had called the men they were going to use (not an overly large group) to the downtown Bureau offices at 3:00 p.m. Finally, Sage telephoned Purvis about 5:30 p.m. to say she would be going to the movies that evening with Hamilton and Dillinger. The problem was that she still did not know which theater it would be, the Marbro or now possibly the Biograph. The fact it might be the Biograph was news to the federal agents. Since the Marbro was playing a Shirley Temple movie, while the Biograph was featuring a gangster film, the Bureau band was quite sure which one Dillinger would choose. So they would recognize her, Sage said that she would be wearing a bright orange skirt.

At 7:15 p.m. Purvis again met with his agents. In a call that afternoon to Chicago, Hoover made it clear he wanted Dillinger taken alive. He feared that in a public place civilians might be hurt and wished no repeat of what had happened at Little Bohemia. What were the orders from Purvis? We know what he said, but the message was mixed. While not directly contradicting his boss's edict, Purvis told his men that Dillinger might or might not be armed and might or might not resist capture. "Don't disgrace the Bureau by letting him get away," he cautioned them. "It is our desire to take him alive, but it will be dangerous." Finally, Purvis told his men, "It will be up to each of you to do whatever you think necessary to protect yourself in taking Dillinger."

Zarkovich then gave the agents an update on what Dillinger looked like—dyed dark hair, pencil-thin mustache, no cleft in the chin, no moles, and a rounder face. He identified the two women Dillinger would be with as an attractive twenty year-old (Hamilton) and a heavier woman in her forties (Sage). Cowley then took one team to the Marbro, while Purvis staked out the Biograph. There was still no word from Sage on which theater it would be. She had been lucky enough to get out of the apartment without raising Dillinger's suspicion with the excuse of needing some butter to cook the chicken. Reaching a telephone she called Purvis with the information he had been waiting for—it would be the Biograph.

Before leaving Sage's apartment, Dillinger counted out stacks of money, rolled them in rubber bands, and placed some of them in his pockets and billfold. Sage guessed the amount to be more than $3,000. Although the Biograph was around the corner from their apartment, Sage, Hamilton, and Dillinger were late for the movie. Dillinger had a loaded .38 Colt handgun in the right rear pocket of his trousers. He wore a straw hat, white shirt and tie, gray slacks, and gold-rimmed glasses. Purvis arrived at the Biograph and inquired as to the time the movie began. It was a few minutes past the 8:30 p.m. starting time and the man he was waiting for, not just this evening, but for months, had still not shown up.

Then, to Purvis's surprise, Dillinger walked up to the ticket window with Hamilton on his arm. Sage was with them wearing, as promised, the orange skirt which looked red under the bright white and pink theater marquee lights. Dillinger bought three tickets and they entered the Biograph. Purvis relayed the information to Cowley and the team at the Marbro. Dillinger's appearance had indeed changed as reported. The famous dimple in his chin had been filled in with tissue from behind his ear, the size of his nose reduced, and his hair was dyed dark brown and his eyebrows had been plucked. There was no doubt, though, on the part of Purvis and his agents that this was the man they had been chasing.

Cowley arrived from the Marbro Theater with agent Charles Winstead. The Texan had been brought in by Hoover as a firearms expert. Winstead was indeed a professional. He had fought in World War I and been an agent with the Bureau since 1926. It was learned later that Winstead and three or four others from the Bureau had been training in Washington, D.C., for just such an opportunity. The Purvis and Cowley Bureau teams were reunited at the Biograph, bringing the total to seventeen federal agents and five East Chicago police. Reassembled, they had been given position assignments by Purvis and Cowley.

At first Purvis considered taking Dillinger inside the theater. But after buying a ticket and entering the packed movie house, he realized that the crowd was too large. Purvis could not even locate Dillinger in the large, dark theater and realized this was no place for a possible shootout. They would have to capture their man

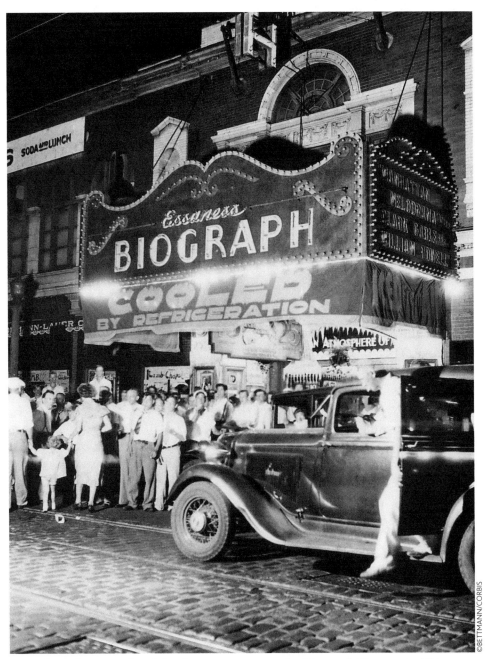

Crowds gather outside of the front entrance to the Biograph Theater in Chicago following the death of Dillinger at the hands of federal agents on July 22, 1934.

outside after the movie. Dillinger and Hamilton had found two seats together on the third row, while Sage sat by herself farther back. Dillinger, according to Hamilton, seemed frisky and carefree that evening. He laughed and joked through the film and repeatedly tried, to Hamilton's embarrassment, to kiss her. Purvis returned to the box office and asked how long the movie would last. The ninety-four-minute film with the previews and newsreels meant the show should be over at 10:35 p.m.

Manhattan Melodrama, starring Clark Gable, Myrna Loy, and William Powell was one of many popular gangster films of the 1930s. Gable plays a gambling racketeer and murderer, not a bank robber. Historian Ellen Poulsen has said of *Manhattan Melodrama* that the Gable character, Blackie Gallagher, was in many ways similar to Dillinger. "He exudes glamour. He's a bad guy with integrity. His character holds a mirror image to the persona that John Dillinger . . . created for the public." Even the names Dillinger and Gallagher are similar. Powell plays Gallagher's childhood friend who ends up prosecuting him. The Powell character closes the film with a summary of crime in America: "Murder without motive seems to be the fashion of the day. And it is just this vicious practice we must stamp out. Crime and criminals became popular. Killers became heroes. Prohibition has gone and these killers who came with it must go with it."

The speech is directed at the crimes surrounding Prohibition. But if the term "bank robberies" replaced Prohibition the meaning could not have been lost on the man sitting in the theater that night with his arm around his girlfriend. Dillinger must have had second thoughts when the racketeer and murderer, played by Gable, goes to the electric chair at the end of the movie. On his way to the chair, the Gable character refuses a commutation to life imprisonment and boldly states, "If I can't live the way I want at least let me die the way I want." Dillinger is said to have sat in his seat after the curtain dropped, lost in thought.

The make-believe world of Hollywood that Sunday night differed from the reality of what was about to take place on the streets of Chicago. Outside the Biograph Theater Cowley had been keeping Hoover constantly informed back in Washington, D.C. The plan remained, even an hour before the movie began, to apprehend Dillinger, not kill him. Yet each agent, as directed by Purvis, had the freedom to take action if the situation got out of hand. Purvis had told his men that the signal to move would be the lighting of his cigar.

While the agents waited for the movie to end, a bizarre episode took place that could have put the whole operation in jeopardy. The frightened manager of the Biograph, having observed too many strange men hanging around his theater, had called the Chicago police. Unaware of what the federal agents and the East Chicago police were up to, the city cops arrived on the scene. With guns pulled they yelled at the federal agents, "Police! Put your hands up!" The agents, who had to show their identification, gave a vague answer for their presence at the theater and sent the city policemen on their way.

By telephone, Hoover once again reminded Cowley to tell his men to take Dillinger alive. But as Purvis had done, the director added that the men should protect themselves. These instructions could be taken two ways. It has been noted that if the plan from the beginning had been to shoot Dillinger, that could have been done as the tickets were being purchased. But this did not happen.

Purvis was as nervous when the show ended at 10:30 p.m. as he was when he arrived two hours before. As he waited on

Dillinger and the two women to emerge, his knees were shaking and his mouth dry as cotton. It was 10:40 p.m. when Dillinger, with Hamilton on his right arm, and Sage following, came out of the theater. He was heard to say, "Boy, wasn't that a great movie?" Standing nearby, Purvis's hands were trembling as he tried to light his cigar to signal the agents. Passing within five feet of Purvis, Dillinger glanced at the agent but then looked away. Since the two men had never met, Dillinger did not recognize him.

Purvis recalled in his autobiography, *American Agent*, the moment when the two men's eyes met as Dillinger walked away from the theater: "I watched him as he moved slowly forward. He looked into my eyes; surely he must have seen something more than casual interest in them, but apparently he didn't recognize me." Hands still shaking, Purvis finally managed to light the cigar. Some have indicated that few agents saw the signal, but Winstead did. "That's Dillinger with the straw hat and glasses," said Winstead to his partner.

Purvis lit the cigar a second time for the other agents to see. The large number of people leaving the theater with Dillinger concerned Purvis. Dillinger turned left and moved south on the sidewalk. Purvis and two or three other agents were now following their quarry and his female companions. While the crowd had to be taken into consideration, at the same time his target was moving farther and farther down the street. Hamilton said that Dillinger had insisted that she take his arm when they walked together. This time, he slipped her arm through his. Sage had moved up and was holding his other arm. Hamilton may have been the first to realize something was up. She grabbed Dillinger to warn him.

Always alert, it did not take Dillinger long to realize that something was not right. He looked over his shoulder and straight

into the eyes of agent Winstead. Two agents were ahead of him
near the alley where Dillinger may have planned to make his escape.
With the agents closing in, there was little doubt that Dillinger
understood he was in a trap. He let loose of the women, crouched,
and started to move. Witnesses differ on whether or not he went
for his gun. Purvis, for one, claimed he saw Dillinger reach into
his pocket. Piquett is one who did not believe that his client would
have shot it out with agents. He believed Dillinger never put up a
fight when outnumbered. However, Dillinger may not have known
that he was outnumbered. The fact that he was in a crowd may also
have given Dillinger reason to think he could get away.

Purvis later said he yelled, "Stick 'em up Johnnie, we've got
you surrounded." Others maintain that no agent warned Dillinger.
Winstead and his two partners did not wait and fired five to
seven bullets. Four of them hit Dillinger, but Winstead's shot was
probably the fatal one. The bullet entered Dillinger's neck, went
through his spine, and then exited below the right eye. All the shots
were from the rear. Dillinger staggered, then fell face first into the
entrance of an alley near the theater. He whispered a few words,
but they were not understandable. Some thought he moved for
two or three minutes, but he was most certainly dead when he hit
the ground. Purvis ran up and took the dead man's pistol, which he
later sent to Hoover.

A mix of frenzy and excitement overtook the crowd. Two women
had been hit in their legs by ricocheting bullets, neither seriously. At
once word spread up and down the street that the man who was shot
and lying in the alley was Dillinger. Shouts of "Dillinger, Dillinger"
rang out from the people along the sidewalks. The crowd, while
electrified by what they had witnessed, was kept under control by the

numerous agents at the scene. Several people managed to approach the place where Dillinger had fallen and dipped handkerchiefs, newspapers, and pieces of cloth into the blood that stained the alley bricks. They became gruesome souvenirs.

As soon as the shooting started, Sage and Hamilton faded into the crowd. Hamilton found safety within the entryway to a store and then reconnected with Sage, who was walking north, the opposite direction the threesome had been headed. As if not knowing what had occurred, Sage asked Hamilton, "What happened?" When about a block away from the scene, the two women tucked their skirts up and ran. Hamilton caught the elevated train at a nearby station, while Sage continued on toward her apartment. Hamilton went to the restaurant where she worked as a waitress and said she would not be in the next day.

Sage reached home and quickly changed out of the infamous "red" skirt that marked her in history as "The Lady in Red." She next located Dillinger's stash of guns. An arsenal might be a more accurate description. There were pistols, a machine gun, bulletproof vests, and an array of ammunition. She wrapped the guns in blankets, hailed a taxi, and probably with the help of her son or a friend, took them to Lake Michigan, where she dumped the lot. Oddly, she then returned to the scene of the shooting. A kid swimming in the lake later recovered the Thompson submachine gun and a bulletproof vest. The Bureau displayed this weapon, which was still in working order decades later, at its Washington, D.C., headquarters.

An ambulance arrived and Dillinger's body was taken to the Alexian Brothers Hospital, where in the parking lot the coroner formally pronounced him dead at 10:50 p.m. The next stop for the corpse was the Cook County Morgue. When informed that night that his son was dead, John Sr. went into shock. First, wondering if there had been a mistake, Dillinger's father said, "Well, John is dead. I thought this had to come and I've been expecting it. At last it happened—the thing I have prayed and prayed would not happen. Are you sure there is no mistake? I want the body brought back here. I'm so sick I can hardly talk. Johnny was not near as bad as he was painted." Later he vented at the authorities for shooting his son down "in cold blood." John Sr. went on to say, "He [Dillinger] was surrounded by 15 men, and that ain't fair. I don't approve of shootin' a man in cold blood." But he added that he, and probably his son, would have preferred for him to be shot rather than captured.

Back in Chicago Dillinger's body was stripped and a tag placed on each big toe with his name and the number 116 for identification. The marker meant this was the 116th body that had reached the morgue during the month of July. Federal fingerprint experts were able to identify him, as the acid procedure on his hands had not worked. In Dillinger's pockets was less than ten dollars (one report said fifty-seven cents), two keys tied with string, and a magazine clipping. Also on the body was a watch with Hamilton's photograph in it and a gold ruby ring inscribed, "With all my love, Polly." That ring ended up missing. Agents took the watch as evidence. The large quantity of cash he was supposedly carrying was never found. Zarkovich has been blamed for taking the cash from Dillinger's body, but there is no proof to that accusation. Several people handled the body or had access to the money that night.

The morgue was in total chaos. One policeman bizarrely decided to shake hands with the corpse. The scene became a revolving door of doctors, nurses, and any gawkers who could talk themselves into

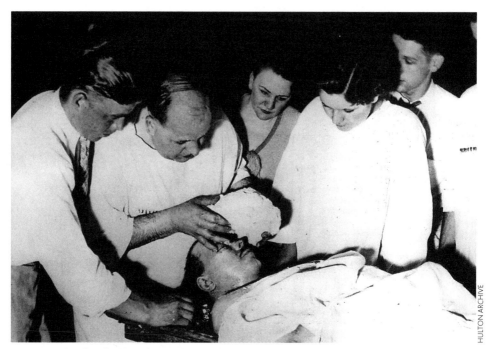

Personnel take the death mask of John Dillinger's face in the morgue in Chicago.

the room. Photographs were taken all night. The autopsy revealed the expected scars from bullet wounds, the attempts at fingerprint removal, and the plastic surgery marks. The brain was removed and then lost. It was eventually recovered, but since there were no abnormalities it was destroyed. John Sr. viewed the taking of his son's brain and other aspects of the autopsy as "mutilations." The only unusual discovery from the autopsy was that Dillinger had rheumatic heart disease.

Powder marks on the body suggested that the shooters were quite close. Two plaster "death mask" casts were made. Before the embalming began, the Chicago undertaker hired by the family asked the coroner to allow the body to be viewed. It was tilted upright behind a glass window and covered with a sheet. An estimated

15,000 individuals filed past in the next few hours. They were representative of the population in general. There were businessmen and high school girls, politicians and housewives, well-dressed professionals and scantily attired nightclub "cuties." While some were eager to have their photographs taken with the body, others became emotional and several looked away once they reached the body. One woman is reported to have said, "He looks like any other dead man, but I guess I'll go through again."

Hoover took a surprisingly low profile on the event in Chicago, making clear that other members of the Dillinger gang were still at large. Attorney General Cummings, however, quickly gave the New Deal and the idea of a federal approach to crime fighting credit for the killing. Careful planning and scientific methods were noted in this encounter on the late-night streets of Chicago. Actually, it was neither Hoover's scientific methods nor Homer Cummings's big government bureaucracy that finally stopped Dillinger. It came down to the old-fashioned, but often successful, method in police work—somebody simply turned him in.

While Hoover remained in the background, attention was now turned on Purvis. After having been in the doghouse with Hoover for the Little Bohemia mess and the dead-end leads he had been following, Purvis now seemed to be the director's new favorite. The morning after the shooting, Hoover gave Purvis a raise and a letter of commendation that read in part, "The shooting and killing of John Dillinger by the Agents of your office under your administrative direction and planning are but another indication of your ability and capacity as a leader and an executive."

Purvis became a national hero, but modestly gave credit to good police work. It was suggested that Cummings go to Chicago to

J. Edgar Hoover (right) congratulates Melvin Purvis upon his arrival in Washington, D.C., on July 25, 1934, a few days after the death of Dillinger, Public Enemy Number One.

congratulate the Bureau team. Cowley, who officially led the agents the night before, was mired in follow-up details to the shooting. Meanwhile, Purvis was having his picture taken with the Attorney General and told of looking into the "killer's eyes." He repeated often the story of lighting his cigar, which set off the deadly chain of events.

While Hoover at first praised Purvis, the national attention was the beginning of the end of his career as an agent. "He Got His Man" blared one Chicago headline. Another read "Purvis is New Type of Sleuth." In what may have been the most damaging story about Purvis, one paper in error called him "Chief of the Federal Bureau of Investigation." This was unacceptable. It was Hoover's Bureau and only he was to receive credit. The seething director became critical of Purvis over minor issues—the agent's phone was busy when he called or Purvis had failed to report where he was every hour. When Hoover visited the Chicago office he found a gun cabinet unlocked and placed a letter of reprimand in Purvis's file.

On Monday morning, July 23, Dillinger's death was the headline on the front page of every newspaper in the nation. The *Chicago American* printed seven photographs of the corpse. As the photographs began to appear, the switch from Dillinger as folk hero to Dillinger as villain began. A New York paper immediately called him "Snake Eyes" for no apparent reason and suggested he had gotten what he deserved. A caption for one photograph referred to the "ice box section of the Chicago morgue" and warned "You Can't Win." This last quote was a reworking of the soon to be familiar "Crime Doesn't Pay" phrase. A San Francisco newspaper called the outlaw the "arch-criminal of the age."

Other newspapers took a different view. The editorials of

newspaper king William Randolph Hearst recklessly criticized the judicial system. It even suggested that shooting down the likes of Dillinger and other outlaws was the "way to deal with them." Some referred to the fact that Dillinger had been shot in "an alley like a rat." The decision by Bureau agents and East Chicago police to take Dillinger on a busy street was questioned. The fact he was shot in the back was seen by some commentators as "Un-American." The idea of Dillinger as the "underdog" appeared in print more than once. Others continued to romanticize him. "Dillinger died as he lived . . . with a smile on his lips and a woman on each arm," wrote one newspaper.

The *Indianapolis Times*, in a special July 23 edition (priced at two cents) led with the huge headline "John Dillinger Slain." The subtexts were titled "Dillinger, Unknown Hoosier Year Ago, Writes Amazing Chapter in Crime History" and "Federal Agents Kill Criminal in Chicago Theater." The articles put together the story of an Indianapolis Quaker's son embittered by a long prison term. His designation as Public Enemy Number One was pointed out, as well as the bloody trail he left behind. The paper stated that as many as fourteen deaths were directly and indirectly tied to him. A drawing of Dillinger in the center of the page is highly flattering, making the bank robber look both attractive and dangerous.

The inquest into Dillinger's death was held the day after the shooting. Federal agent Cowley, still doing the heavy lifting in the case, gave testimony at the hearing that Dillinger had drawn his weapon and was shot "before he could get the gun into the firing position." The jury returned a quick verdict of justifiable homicide. Winstead, the actual shooter, was not present and neither was Sage the informant. No question was raised as to why Dillinger and so many lawmen were all present at the same place. The fact that all the bullet wounds on the body were from behind was neither noted nor explored.

There has been much speculation as to why there was no attempt to take Dillinger alive. The lawmen did, after all, have a large force of men and the element of surprise on their side. Since there had been rumors that certain members of the East Chicago Police Department had been in Dillinger's pay, they may not have wanted him talking. Two eyewitnesses, not called at the inquest, told reporters that the agents stepped up very close to Dillinger and fired at him point blank in the back. Powder burns on the victim's clothes support this story. Could the shooting then be called an assassination? Author Dary Matera in his book *John Dillinger:*

Dillinger's father, John Sr., at left, and the outlaw's half brother, Hubert, wait to claim their relative's body in Chicago.

The Life and Death of America's First Celebrity Criminal repeatedly referred to Dillinger's shooting as an "assassination" and also called it an "execution."

By definition an assassination is a sudden or secret attack on an important person for political or other reasons. From the evidence at the scene, and what is known about the plan that evening, the shooting of Dillinger was not an assassination. The main reason for such a conclusion is that both Hoover and Purvis had given orders that he be taken alive. Winstead, the man who fired the fatal shot, was a veteran lawman. But even professionals can get emotionally caught up in a hazardous situation. Winstead may not have been afraid of the outlaw, but many were. Dillinger had been accused of killing at least one man, had taken part in violent shootouts, and had used weapons in his robberies and escapes. To use a familiar phrase, he was always "armed and dangerous." Dillinger probably could have been taken alive, but that will never be proven.

John Sr. was soon on his way to Chicago to bring his son back to Indianapolis. A few claimed that they did not think the corpse was really Dillinger. When John Sr. saw the body, however, he cried, "My boy." Other family members also made a positive identification. When the Mooresville undertaker arrived, the body was placed in the hearse for the two hundred-mile journey back to Indianapolis. Curiosity knew no limits when it came to Dillinger. Another 5,000 people looked on as the casket was taken away. John Sr., his son, Hubert, and the editor of the Mooresville newspaper accompanied the body. While the Hoosier state song is not "Back Home Again in Indiana," (that distinction goes to "On the Banks of the Wabash, Far Away,") Dillinger was now making his final trip back to the Hoosier State.

11

Back Home in Indiana

The body of John Dillinger arrived in Mooresville, Indiana, on Tuesday, July 24, 1934. Crowds had lined the highways as the hearse made its way from Chicago through Indiana. Due to thousands wishing to view the body, the Harvey Funeral Home had two showings the day before the body was moved to the home of Dillinger's sister, Audrey Hancock. She lived on the south side of Indianapolis in the Maywood neighborhood. Audrey did not believe the body was that of her brother until she was shown a scar on his leg. Seeing the wound from the Saint Paul, Minnesota, getaway the previous April convinced her.

The Mooresville mortician did extensive cosmetic work in order to make the body presentable. The exit wound of the bullet beneath the right eye had caused disfigurement on that side of the face. The casket was a modest $165 model. John Sr. purchased a new gray suit, white shirt, and polka-dot tie for his son. He had been offered $10,000 to "lend" his son's body for a circuit of viewing, but refused. The cost of the funeral pressed John Sr.'s finances. Whatever money his son had amassed over the past year had all disappeared after the shooting.

When the body arrived in Maywood on Wednesday, July 25, a circus atmosphere surrounded Audrey's home. The neighborhood was filled with people, and cars were parked for blocks along the streets. Temporary stands selling soft drinks had been set up and the lawn was flooded with gawkers and alleged mourners. The police finally had to cordon off the area, letting only select individuals into the Hancock home. The Great Depression was a time of boredom for most people with many looking for entertainment. Large and unruly crowds were drawn by the homegrown crook who had become a national celebrity. There was even a rumor that Baby Face Nelson might make an appearance to pay his last respects. This, of course, did not happen.

Two ministers presided over a Christian service, although there is no evidence that Dillinger gave much thought to religion. Hymns were sung, but there were no eulogies or sermons, just prayers. Audrey fainted and among the family there were tears all around. Journalists and photographers filled the lawn outside the Hancock home. An airplane was taking pictures from above. Back in Chicago an epitaph had been written in chalk outside the Biograph Theater:

> Stranger, stop and wish me well,
> Just say a prayer for my soul in Hell.
> I was a good fellow, most people said,
> Betrayed by a woman all dressed in red.

While the burial was scheduled for Thursday, July 26, the family made the decision to bury the man who was their son, brother, and uncle that Wednesday. It fooled some, but not all. A crowd of thousands made their way to Indianapolis's Crown Hill Cemetery on the city's north side. A severe thunderstorm did little to deter the throngs from attempting to witness the interment. Dillinger was finally lowered into a grave in the large cemetery that held a president of the United States, three vice-presidents, two Indiana governors, several senators, and beloved Hoosier Poet James Whitcomb Riley. The grave was guarded by police for a week. To make sure there would be no body snatching, John Sr. had the grave covered in steel and concrete. Although no gravestone was placed on the site for two years, when one was erected it was soon vandalized by souvenir seekers. Later two other headstones were also destroyed. (In the 1990s a woman with no connection to Dillinger asked to be buried close to him. Crown Hill found a plot for her within one hundred feet.)

Six weeks after Dillinger's death, his family was appearing on the stage of the Lyric Theater in downtown Indianapolis and later went on the road to retell their story. Large crowds eager to hear their tales paid twenty-five cents for the matinees and forty cents

A crowd gathers outside E. F. Harvey's Funeral Service in Mooresville, Indiana, where Dillinger's body was taken after being gunned down in Chicago.

for the evening shows. It is reported that audiences were respectful. The theme was always "Crime Does Not Pay," but clearly most patrons of the shows were there to hear about the crimes and the man who committed them. Dillinger's last visit to the Mooresville farm in April was the central part of the story.

John Sr. later joined Emil Wanatka at Little Bohemia in Wisconsin for shows, but interest eventually waned. Billie Frechette and other gang molls sold their stories to newspapers and magazines. The Dillinger "business" was also profitable for those who had "souvenirs." These were often grisly items from the shooting, including handkerchiefs and cloths stained with dried blood. Bricks from the alley near the Biograph were auctioned off, as well as the clothes Dillinger was wearing the night he died.

In the days and weeks after the burial new stories emerged, many from the Bureau of Investigation headquarters in Washington, D.C. J. Edgar Hoover, at first strangely quiet on the event, called Dillinger a "yellow rat" and said his agency was now moving on to capture others just like him. Baby Face Nelson became the new Public Enemy Number One. The Bureau was also on the lookout for Homer Van Meter. Mistakenly, the already dead John Hamilton's name was also placed on the most-wanted list.

Most of Dillinger's gang and a number of those associated with him quickly followed their leader to the grave. Although not a gang member, the first was James Probasco, the man who had hid Dillinger during his plastic surgery. In late July he apparently jumped from a nineteen-story window in Chicago while under police custody. Some have contended he was being held out of the window by his ankles to encourage him to talk. But, as with many stories surrounding Dillinger, it is impossible to know the truth.

Van Meter, Dillinger's faithful sidekick over much of the past year, was next. He was trailed on August 23 by four policemen and cornered in a Saint Paul neighborhood. He was to fall dead in an alley just like his friend. This time there was a hail of more than fifty bullets by the city's police force. Van Meter attempted to shield his face, only to have his fingers shredded by the bullets. Having placed Van Meter high on his list, Hoover was upset he had not been in on the raid. One reason for the director's response was that a Congressional committee had pressed him as to whether he had ever personally captured a criminal. He had not, but eventually would be in on the capture of another high-profile crook, Alvin Karpis.

The next month, Charles Makley and Harry Pierpont, awaiting execution in Ohio, imitated Dillinger's famous ploy by making two fake guns in their prison cells. When they tried to use them

A small crowd gathers near Dillinger's burial place, next to his mother, at Crown Hill Cemetery in Indianapolis, circa 1934.

on September 23, Makley was shot and killed. Pierpont, also shot in the attempted breakout, survived only to be electrocuted on October 17. Pierpont was buried in Indianapolis and Van Meter's body was returned to Fort Wayne, Indiana.

Nelson made it five deaths in five straight months. In a shootout with two federal agents, Samuel Cowley and H. E. Hollis, Nelson killed both men. They had both been on the Dillinger assignment that July night at the Biograph in Chicago. Six Bureau agents had been killed by this time, half of them by Nelson. While seriously wounded (he was hit an estimated dozen times), Baby Face escaped with his wife, Helen, and an associate. His body was later found dumped near Chicago. Helen was later caught and sent to prison in Michigan. When asked how a woman could leave her children with relatives to follow an outlaw who was certain to be caught, she gave a simple answer. "Well, I knew that Les didn't have very long to live and I wanted to be with him just as long as I could." Relatives raised the Nelsons' son and daughter until their mother was released.

Dillinger's lawyer, Louis Piquett, spent time in federal prison for harboring or protecting Van Meter, who was never his client. Piquett was, ironically, found not guilty of assisting and hiding Dillinger, who was his client. The attorney's involvement with Dillinger was always puzzling. In addition to never being paid well for his services, his ongoing association with the outlaw might today be considered obstruction of justice. When Piquett failed to regain his attorney's license after his two years in prison, he took up bartending. He received a pardon from President Harry S Truman in 1951 and died the following year.

Indiana State Police Director Matt Leach continued to be obsessed with the Dillinger case. The exact nature of the "case" was never clear. It may have been an attempt to tie East Chicago police to Dillinger. Leach told an Indiana newspaper in 1935 that Dillinger never had a good-looking girlfriend because the outlaw was not that attractive to women. In a racist comment he said that Dillinger only appealed to "half-breed Indians" such as Billie Frechette and Polly Hamilton. Hoover, tired of Leach, may have used his influence to have him fired from his Indiana post in 1937.

Leach went on to serve in World War II as he had in World War I. Leach only met Dillinger twice, both times when others had captured him. He wrote a book about the man he had chased across the country, but it was never published. Leach and his wife were killed in a car accident in 1955 while returning home to Indiana from New York. In a bizarre turn of events, the trip was in connection with a possible television show about Dillinger. It could be said that while Leach never got Dillinger, in the end, Dillinger got him.

An unlikely victim of the Dillinger case was agent Melvin Purvis. Months after Dillinger's death he led the manhunt for Charles Floyd that ended in Pretty Boy's death on an Ohio farm October 22, 1934. He was one of several men who pumped dozens of bullets into the fugitive. "You are Pretty Boy Floyd," said Purvis. The dying man replied with a sneer, "I'm Charles Arthur Floyd." The Floyd shooting, which should have been viewed as another success for the agency, was only seen by the director as an additional boost for Purvis. Purvis had earlier made a number of headline-capturing comments about going after Nelson that outraged Hoover. The star agent was reported in the papers to have also said, "If it's the last thing I do, I'll get Baby Face Nelson." He did not. But Purvis received more publicity than the director and such grandstanding, as Hoover viewed it, could not continue. He soon turned on his celebrated agent. Hoover ordered Purvis back to Chicago and told him to lay low.

One biographer has called Purvis's treatment by Hoover harassment. He was sent on useless tours and given low priority assignments. (Hoover was known to send those who fell out of favor with him to offices as far from Washington, D.C., as possible.) The point was that no individual, other than Hoover, could be given sole hero status in the Bureau. It could be a team operation or a Hoover operation, but never one agent's operation. Although Charles Winstead no doubt fired the fatal bullet at Dillinger, even his role was buried. The agency's line was that it was a group operation that brought Dillinger down.

The title of Alston Purvis's biography of his father is *The Vendetta: FBI Hero Melvin Purvis's War against Crime, and J. Edgar Hoover's War against Him*, which states exactly what the son thought about the director. The dictionary defines a vendetta as a "feud marked by bitter hostility." This would be accurate as there was much animosity by each man toward the other. No doubt because of these bad relations with Hoover, Purvis quit the agency almost one year after Dillinger's death. Purvis served in World War II and was then involved in various business ventures. In 1960 at his South Carolina home, Purvis's gun went off and a bullet entered his brain from under his chin. Alston leaves open the idea that it could have been an accident. The gun was not one his father often used, but he may possibly have been cleaning it. Although not in good health he had much to live for. The gun was a Colt .45 given to Purvis by his fellow Bureau agents upon his resignation.

Hoover ignored Purvis's passing. In its 1956 official history, *The F.B.I. Story*, Purvis was not mentioned. There is little doubt that leaving Purvis out was no accident, due, no doubt, to jealousy on Hoover's part. Purvis did not mention Hoover in his book *American Agent* in 1936. The feud has continued. Alston concludes that Hoover's fifty year "fiefdom" of the agency and the secret files he kept on presidents and civil rights leaders made him "perhaps a more villainous figure than the gangsters he pursued."

Winstead, who is credited with firing the shot that killed Dillinger, also left the Bureau in 1943 after a run-in with Hoover. He tried to rejoin the agency after World War II, but Hoover would not allow it. He died in New Mexico in 1973 at the age of eighty-two. Hoover died the year before Winstead, in 1972. Never retiring as director and feared by presidents for what he knew about them, Hoover always used his connection to Dillinger to build his image. Up until his own death he considered Dillinger's death his greatest success.

Richard Gid Powers has written that Hoover was so gripped by Dillinger that forty years later he talked about his rival as if he were still alive. Beginning in 1937 Hoover's office, said Powers, was turned into a kind of unofficial Dillinger museum. Dillinger memorabilia included one of the death masks of the criminal, the gun he was carrying that night, his straw hat, and even the coins and woman's photograph that were in his pockets. *The New Yorker* magazine wrote of Dillinger's "startling white plaster . . . death mask" staring "empty-eyed from under the glass display case" outside Hoover's office. Hoover's 1938 book, *Persons in Hiding*, did not hold back in stating what the director really thought about Dillinger—a murderer, a rat, and other unpleasant references. A recent, now retired, Bureau director has said, "Hoover had a thing about Dillinger. The older he got, the more he talked about Dillinger. He would talk on and on about this stuff."

The 2011 film *J. Edgar* makes it appear that the capture of Bruno Hauptmann, convicted kidnapper of aviator Charles Lindbergh's infant son, "made" the Bureau the institution it became. In truth it was the eighteen-month pursuit of Great Depression-era kidnappers and bank robbers, and especially the death of Dillinger, that assured the Bureau's fame. Hoover's agency needed a celebrity off of whom to play and it had that in Dillinger. The director clearly realized this, which could account for his lifelong obsession.

Anna Sage, the "Lady in Red," received only $5,000 of the $25,000 Dillinger reward. She also ended up being deported to Romania, just what she had been trying to avoid when she gave the Bureau Dillinger. She died in her native country in 1947. Claire Bond Potter concluded in her book *Don't Call Us Molls* that Sage may have been given too much credit for bringing about Dillinger's end. While she did finger the Hoosier public enemy, Potter contends there were others who wanted to get rid of Dillinger. These include Chicago gangsters, who were being hurt by the attention Dillinger was drawing to other criminal activity in their city. Alleged corrupt law officials also were more than happy to see Dillinger out of the picture. And federal agents, especially Hoover, wanted to nail him for the publicity and glory it would bring to the rising agency. "Not scientific policing but a more capable local network of politicians, police, mobsters, and criminal workers produced Dillinger at the Biograph Theater on Sunday, July 22," wrote Potter.

After her release from prison, Evelyn "Billie" Frechette, Dillinger's main moll, went on to give talks at carnivals about her boyfriend. Dillinger's last moll, Polly Hamilton, stayed in Chicago. Both women died of cancer in 1969, one month apart. Dillinger's ex-wife, Beryl Hovious, died in Mooresville, Indiana, in 1993 at the age of eighty-seven. Martin Zarkovich, of the East Chicago police and Sage's ex-boyfriend, also died in 1993. As federal agents were not allowed to collect reward money, it is assumed that Zarkovich and his East Chicago colleagues may have received the cash that Sage did not.

Immediately after the death, execution, and capture of the major outlaws in 1934, Hoover's publicity machine went all out to revise the story of the Dillinger shooting. The tale was devised by Rex Collier, under Hoover's direction, and published in a syndicated, six-part newspaper feature. First, according to Collier, Hoover had directed the Dillinger operation from Washington that hot night in July. It was the agency's scientific methods that

LIBRARY OF CONGRESS

J. Edgar Hoover signs autographs for fans, circa 1940. Hoover remained as FBI director until his death from a heart attack at his home in Washington, D.C., on May 2, 1972.

had led to the shooting. Sage was mentioned, but then reduced in importance. Collier even added that Dillinger feared the agency, attempting to make the dead outlaw look "chicken" when dealing with the federal agents. The Bureau's familiar line became "the FBI always got its man."

Hollywood did not wait long to reflect the change in public opinion. Again, the shift from Dillinger as Robin Hood to Dillinger as public menace was promoted by Hoover and the Bureau's publicity arm. A year after Dillinger's death James Cagney (who four years before played the villain in *Public Enemies*) was cast in the role of a Bureau hero in the film *G-Men*. Cagney represented what Hoover wanted represented—a new kind of lawman who was intelligent, college-educated, and used scientific methods to solve crimes. The 1935 film placed teamwork over the individual and stressed the use of fingerprints, microscopes, and agents trained in boxing, judo, and the use of firearms.

The plot of *G-Men* mirrored much of what had occurred the previous two years. The three fictional hoodlums in the film were based in part on Nelson, Floyd, and Dillinger. While all part of one gang in the movie the three outlaw characters are not nearly as successful as their real-life counterparts. The Little Bohemia-like raid does not make the federal agents look inept. Agents are not confused, no agent is killed, and when the Dillinger character escapes it is not the Bureau's fault. When "Dillinger" is later killed it is to avenge the murder of Cagney's girlfriend. Since the motion picture industry had ordered that "no picture on the life or exploits of John Dillinger be produced, distributed, or exhibited," the movie *G-Men* pushed this boundary with its story and characters.

Collier, who had written the first history of the hunt for

Dillinger, from Hoover's point of view, also produced the radio series "G-Men." Listeners tuned in to the first show on July 20, 1935, almost one year to the day after the event at the Biograph Theater. The first story was "The Life and Death of John Dillinger." The show, as had the articles by Collier, depicted Dillinger as a scared and hopeless man. One piece of dialogue has him saying, "What's the difference? Ain't the G-Men hot on me—I can't sleep— they're everywhere—might as well croak now, if you can't get them off my trail." The Purvis character is given a different name. Those glued to their radio heard at the end of the program that twenty-six people who had helped or been associated with Dillinger were either dead or in prison.

A year after the Cagney film, the Collier newspaper series, and several radio programs, Hoover approved an official Bureau comic strip titled "War on Crime." The 1936 comic strip has Dillinger being shot from the front and the credit given to the agency's scientific methods. One cartoon panel has a Hoover-like figure showing visitors the glass display case of Dillinger souvenirs. All the men have their hats off. Hoover was said to have loved comics, even the fictional and popular Dick Tracy. Comics, believed Hoover, were the best vehicle to reach Great Depression youth. While never the title character, Dillinger has appeared in a dozen other crime-related comic books since 1936.

Hoover continued to beat the drums for his new agency, taking credit for what had become a string of successes. In a speech in December 1934, as the momentous year of crime came to an end, the director said, "John Dillinger, the flag-bearer of lawlessness, is dead, killed by federal bullets. Pretty Boy Floyd lies in his grave, dead of gunshot wounds . . . by our special agents. The career of

Baby Face Nelson is over . . . ending his filthy [life]." Hoover noted that each met their end as a result of his federal agency and their agents. Hoover did not accept the excuse of "young Johnny's" raw deal for the botched, small-time robbery in Mooresville in 1924.

Dillinger is gone now, as are those who either rode with him or pursued him. But the larger than life bank robber of the 1930s left a legend and legacy. Since his death the word "legend" has been used in connection with Dillinger. There are several reasons for this fame or notoriety. In part it has to do with his appealing personality and quick wit. Even if they did not agree with his bank robbing and violence, people liked to read about him. He was also considered a good-looking man who usually behaved in a gentlemanly manner as he went about his criminal work.

Another element that has kept the Dillinger legacy alive are his numerous and remarkable escapes. The unbelievable breakout from the Crown Point jail and successful getaway from the lodge in northern Wisconsin added to the lore. The way he eluded the law lent him what some called a Robin Hood style—an inability to be caught and giving to the poor what he took from the rich. This was in spite of the fact that Dillinger was not known, other than his family, to have shared his ill-gotten gains with the poor. The fact that he robbed banks—institutions not well thought of during the Great Depression—added to his celebrity.

For all of Dillinger's personal attributes, it seemed the public often lost sight of the fact that people around him, on both sides of the law, were shot and sometimes killed. Dillinger biographer Elliot Gorn reminds those caught up in the Robin Hood mystique that the bank robber traveled with "a gang of talented murderers." The Dillinger family continues to refute the East Chicago, Indiana, shooting of Officer William O'Malley by their famous relative. Yet, numerous witnesses were ready to testify against him in Crown Point had he not escaped. Harry Pierpont and Charles Makley were both convicted of the murder of Lima sheriff Jess Sarber. While never indicted or convicted, the evidence against Baby Face Nelson for multiple killings is well documented. Dillinger knew the kind of life he was leading. "The world's a very dangerous place," he once joked, "few get out of it alive." The final conversations with his father and sister in April 1934 seemed to confirm that he knew how it would all end.

Another reason for the Dillinger legend has been that it all seemed a throwback to the romantic and exciting days of the Old West. Fifty years had passed since the heyday of the likes of Jesse James, Billy the Kid, the Dalton Gang, and other Old West bank robbers. The last job Dillinger was planning was a train robbery, the main activity of Butch Cassidy and the Sundance Kid. The public saw in Dillinger similarities to these well-known figures of the past. Robbing banks was not a new occupation in 1933. It still occurs today, but with less fanfare and less success. But Dillinger brought with it a new style. The clothes he and his gang wore were flashy, the cars they drove were sleek and fast, and the guns they used were loud and dangerous. And whether they were glamorous or not, there always seemed to be women around them.

There is the legend of Dillinger and there is also the legacy. Some have called the fourteen months of Dillinger's rampage in the Midwest the "reign of terror." Gorn's book is titled *Dillinger's Wild Ride*. But while being the most famous, he was not the only bank robber to capture the nation's attention. The two years of 1933 and 1934 saw an epidemic of high-profile crooks who wreaked havoc in Great Depression-era America. As a result, changes came about in law enforcement practices and government roles in fighting crime. "The myth and romance associated with Dillinger . . . should not obscure the important role he played in pointing out the deficiencies in law enforcement," according to Indiana historian James H. Madison. "Dillinger made a mockery of small-town banks, local police, and county sheriffs." Madison indicated that Leach was under great limitations in dealing with the outlaw, adding that as a result few looked to the state police for help in dealing with the bandit. He also noted that no one even thought to call Leach when Dillinger escaped from the Crown Point jail.

Lawmen on the local, state, and federal levels realized that they had to match or exceed the technology being used by the criminals. For state and local police this included the use of two-way radios, securing faster automobiles, and equipping their officers with bulletproof vests. In addition they needed armored cars and tank-like vehicles to use in raids. Eventually police outfitted their men with weapons that equaled those being used against them. Pistols were replaced with automatic weapons and powerful rifles. The training of crime fighters became more professional.

Even the facilities that housed criminals were enhanced to provide better protection for those inside, both lawmen and lawbreakers. Jails, police headquarters, and prisons were all upgraded. In banks, increased armed guards, sophisticated vaults, and better protected teller cages were installed. Teller cages were either made higher or rails were added to stop Dillinger-like bounding over the counters. Dary Matera in his book *John Dillinger: The Life and Death of America's First Celebrity Criminal* lists other ways the man from Mooresville was responsible for altering crime fighting. These included the arming of firemen and the use of National Guard troops, tanks, and aircraft. There were also attempts to curb the popular press from glorifying gangsters and criminals as celebrities and heroes.

At a time when the federal government was handling new and numerous economic problems arising from the Great Depression, it was doing the same in the arena of law enforcement. In 1935 the Bureau (or Division) of Investigation became the Federal Bureau of Investigation or FBI, another of the many "Alphabet Agencies" of President Franklin D. Roosevelt's New Deal. Yet even when federal authority was viewed as effective and valuable in law enforcement, concern over too much power in the hands of Washington, D.C., was raised. The politics of state versus federal power and how these two entities worked with each other became issues both then and on into the future.

Bryan Burrough in his book *Public Enemies: America's Greatest Crime Wave and the Birth of the FBI, 1933–34* asked if the Dillinger-era "War on Crime" was merely a way for Hoover to create another new and powerful New Deal agency. Burrough answers his own question: "The F.B.I. did not invent Dillinger in order to become a national police agency—Dillinger was already on the scene offering the F.B.I. the opportunity to become what Hoover envisioned. In fact, the Lindbergh Law required the F.B.I. to pursue alleged kidnappers and killers. The idea of an agency such as the F.B.I. fit well into the design of many New Dealers."

The string of successful encounters between major crime figures and high-profile federal agents and officials such as Purvis and Hoover made G-Men synonymous with being the "good guys." David Ruth in his book *Inventing the Public Enemy: The Gangster in American*

Culture, 1918–1934 called Dillinger "the most important" outlaw of the time. Ruth added that Dillinger served to make the FBI what it became—a national crime-fighting power. By fashioning Dillinger, Nelson, and other bandits as the "bad guys," Hoover demonstrated the effectiveness of the federal government as a force for right against criminals bent on doing harm to the public.

As the FBI increased its use of technology, so, too, did local and state crime enforcement agencies. Scientific methods and procedures were soon brought into play by crime investigators across the country. Crime scene and physical evidence, such as fingerprints, blood types, tire tracks, and even clues found on personal items, were all used to track down suspects. Scientific techniques were modern and therefore, by using such procedures, the FBI looked modern.

Bureau agents, due to new federal legislation, could now carry guns, cross state lines, and make arrests. In effect they became a national police force. This was to be a force for good in most cases over the years. As with any bureaucracy, there have been critics who have maintained that at times the FBI overstepped its authority. Whether it did so in the demise of John Dillinger is debatable. What is certain is that the Bureau, by being a national police force, allowed its resources to offset any advantage criminals may have held in the early 1930s.

There has never really been an end to the Dillinger story. He lives on in books, films, and a museum. In 1970 Jay Robert Nash and Ron Offen wrote in their book *Dillinger, Dead or Alive?* that Dillinger was "still out there." The theme of the fictional films *Lady in Red* and *Dillinger and Capone* are both that Dillinger got away and the Bureau shot the wrong man. A few writers and speculators have maintained that the story put out by the Bureau that they had killed Dillinger was merely a cover-up.

The fascination with Dillinger has never stopped. Cars he drove and guns he owned continue to draw attention. A 1933 Essex Terraplane was expensively restored in 2001 by a collector, and there is one on display in the East Chicago, Indiana, Dillinger Museum. In 2012 a 1930 Model A Ford, probably the car that Dillinger and Hamilton used the night of the Little Bohemia raid, sold for $165,000. A Thompson machine gun that Dillinger had stolen in his Crown Point jail break was returned to Lake County Indiana in 2001 by the FBI at the direction of Director Louis Freeh.

There are also examples of how Dillinger has found his way into the popular new arena of public history. This includes tours of Dillinger sites and the Dillinger Museum. Historian Gorn's book

COURTESY MARTY N. DAVIS

Dillinger's marker at Crown Hill Cemetery is a popular place for visitors, who often leave behind coins and take chips of the marker for souvenirs.

describes a mix of public history and tourism with what he has called "The Dillinger Trail." In 1994 the *Chicago Tribune* charted places for tourists to visit that included Little Bohemia in upstate Wisconsin, where Dillinger and Melvin Purvis shot it out; the Crown Point Jail, where Dillinger escaped with a wooden gun; the Biograph Theater in Chicago, where Dillinger met his end; and Crown Hill Cemetery in Indianapolis, where Dillinger is buried. The Dillinger grave remains the most asked-for site at the cemetery.

Then there is the Dillinger Museum. A collection of Dillinger memorabilia was sold in 1996 to the Lake County Indiana Convention and Visitors Bureau for $400,000. The county paid $1 million to a company that specialized in professional exhibitions to create a new museum on an interstate highway near the Illinois and Indiana border. Just before it opened, the county sheriff asked whether this was not a monument to a "criminal and cop killer." Crown Point, the site of Dillinger's jail escape, is located in Lake County. The Dillinger family then sued the museum, claiming that their relative was never officially charged or convicted of murder. (He actually was charged with the murder, but never stood trial.) This closed the exhibition down for almost ten years, with the case finally settled out of court. The museum, which opened in 2008, has a variety of artifacts and memorabilia from Dillinger and his times.

Even the FBI has kept Dillinger alive. The Bureau's Academy in Quantico, Virginia, has a mock town on its training grounds. It is called Hogan's Alley. A park in the Academy is named Tall Pines in reference to Little Bohemia and the trees of northern Wisconsin through which Dillinger escaped. Hogan's Alley has a replica of the Biograph Theater. On the marquee is *Manhattan Melodrama* starring Clark Gable and Myrna Loy just like that night in Chicago decades ago.

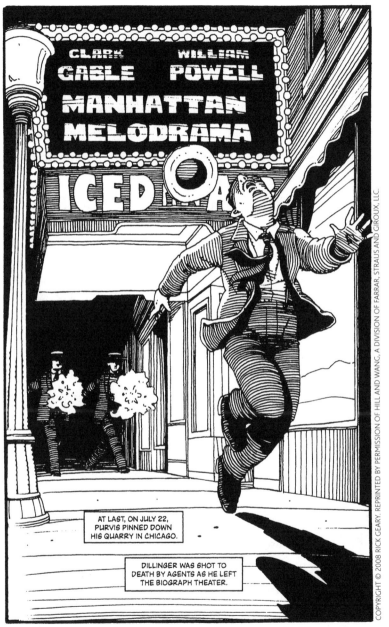

Cartoonist Richard Geary imagines the scene at the Biograph Theater when John Dillinger was gunned down by federal agents for his 2008 book J. Edgar Hoover: A Graphic Biography, *one of the many ways Dillinger still lives in American popular culture.*

The title never changes. Guns owned by Dillinger, Bonnie and Clyde, and Nelson have at times been kept at Quantico. Some guns still work and agents have even shot the weapons. One observer has noted that life-size human targets on the pistol range look a bit like Dillinger.

Most historians and biographers have been careful not to praise Dillinger or make him too appealing. Others, such as Ralph de Toledano, have written admiringly of him. De Toledano noted that Dillinger's intelligence could have made him a success in a number of professions. The Dillinger family is the most protective of his reputation. They have told their side of the story in Carol Sissom's book *Banking with Dillinger*. Its theme is again the familiar "Crime Does Not Pay." But the justifications are so plentiful that the issue of whether Dillinger was really a "bad guy" at all is left open to question by the book.

A great-nephew attributes his ancestor's life of crime to the long sentence he was given in 1924: "He told his father that he was treated like an animal in prison and that they had taken nine years of his and they owed him." This defense, along with denials of his guilt on a variety of charges, is often given by the family and others. The strongest denial is over the O'Malley shooting in East Chicago. Relatives insist that Mary Kinder, Pierpont's girlfriend, provided a legitimate alibi for Dillinger. But being part of the gang, however well she knew him, may not make her the most reliable witness. She claimed that the money found on Dillinger from the East Chicago robbery was planted by the police in Tucson, Arizona. Numerous eyewitnesses to the East Chicago shooting were ready to testify against Dillinger in Crown Point. And the lawmen in Arizona could not have acquired the numbered bills from Indiana so quickly after his arrest and placed them on their prisoner. In addition, Tucson officials had no motive to frame Dillinger.

Alston Purvis, son of Melvin Purvis, captured this conflict over how Dillinger is viewed when he wrote, "No criminal had ever been like him, so bold, so unafraid of the law. He was both feared and—for his audacity—reluctantly admired." The books on Dillinger keep coming, as do Hollywood and documentary portrayals of him. There have been four theatrical depictions of Dillinger and his yearlong journey that included robberies, escapes, shootouts, and his death. Television movies have been made. There have also been songs and artistic renderings of the outlaw. Some glamorize the havoc he wreaked, while others condemn him. Even movies that were not about Dillinger reminded people of him. More than one biographer has noted his uncanny resemblance to the popular and rising movie star of the 1930s, Humphrey Bogart. Fictional accounts of Dillinger and his gang can be found in the novels *Mad Dog* by Jack Kelly and *Handsome Harry* by James Carlos Blake.

The various Dillinger gangs have been credited with stealing close to a half million dollars when their robberies are added together. A dollar amount, though, cannot be placed on the cost in terms of human life. Twenty-two men (eleven lawmen and eleven outlaws, including Dillinger) were killed or executed during the 1933 and 1934 bank robber's rampage in the Midwest. Six or more civilians, usually bystanders at robberies, lost their lives. The wounded numbered in the dozens.

Most of all, Dillinger lives on in the public imagination. Jeffrey King's book *The Rise and Fall of the Dillinger Gang* ends with the line, "Never again will the likes of the Dillinger Gang be seen in America." The *Chicago Tribune* may have best captured the spirit of the legacy of the long-dead Dillinger. The newspaper did so the day after his death. No outlaw in American history, the newspaper wrote, "ever so captured the imagination of the public." It could be added that no public crime figure since Dillinger has either.

Learn More about John Dillinger and His Times

Books

Beverly, William. *On the Lam: Narratives of Flight in J. Edgar Hoover's America*. Jackson, MS: University Press of Mississippi, 2008.

Bolden, Tonya. *FDR's Alphabet Soup: New Deal America, 1932–1939*. New York: Alfred A. Knopf, 2010.

Brinkley, Alan. *American History: Connecting with the Past*. New York: McGraw Hill, 2012.

Burrough, Bryan. *Public Enemies: America's Greatest Crime Wave and the Birth of the FBI, 1933–34*. New York: Penguin Press, 2004.

Cromie, Robert, and Joseph Pinkston. *Dillinger: A Short and Violent Life*. Evanston, IL: Chicago Historical Bookworks, 1990.

de Toledano, Ralph. *J. Edgar Hoover: The Man and His Time*. New Rochelle, NY: Arlington House, 1973.

Geary, Rick. *J. Edgar Hoover: A Graphic Biography*. New York: Hill and Wang, 2008.

Gentry, Curt. *J. Edgar Hoover: The Man and His Secrets*. New York: W. W. Norton, 1991.

Girardin, G. Russell, and William J. Helmer. *Dillinger: The Untold Story*. Bloomington: Indiana University Press, 2005.

Gorn, Elliot J. *Dillinger's Wild Ride*. New York: Oxford University Press, 2009.

Helmer, William J., and Rick Mattix. *The Complete Public Enemy Almanac*. Nashville, TN: Cumberland House, 2007.

Helmer, William J., and Steven Nickel. *Baby Face Nelson: Portrait of a Public Enemy*. Nashville, TN: Cumberland House, 2002.

Hill, Traci L. *Thompson, the American Legend: The First Submachine Gun*. Cobourg, Ontario: Collector Grade Publications, 1996.

Kessler, Ronald. *The Secrets of the FBI*. New York: Crown Publishers, 2011.

Kennedy, David M. *Freedom from Fear: The American People in Depression and War, 1929–1945*. New York: Oxford University Press, 1999.

King, Jeffery S. *The Rise and Fall of the Dillinger Gang*. Nashville, TN: Cumberland House, 2005.

Kyle, Chris, with William Doyle. *American Gun: A History of the U.S. in Ten Firearms*. New York: William Morrow, 2013.

Lounderback, Lew. *The Bad Ones: Gangsters of the '30s and Their Molls*. Greenwich, CT: Fawcett, 1968.

Maccabbee, Paul. *John Dillinger Slept Here: A Crook's Tour of Crime and Corruption in Saint Paul, 1920–1936*. Saint Paul: Minnesota Historical Society Press, 1995.

Madison, James H. *The Indiana Way: A State History*. Bloomington: Indiana University Press, 1990.

_____. *Indiana through Tradition and Change: 1920–1945*. Indianapolis: Indiana Historical Society, 1982.

Manchester, William. *The Glory and the Dream: A Narrative History of America, 1932–1972*. Boston: Little, Brown, and Company, 1973.

Matera, Dary. *John Dillinger: The Life and Death of America's First Celebrity Criminal*. New York: Carroll and Graf Publishers, 2004.

Nash, Jay Robert, and Ron Offen. *Dillinger, Dead or Alive?* Chicago: Regnery, 1970.

Olsen, Marilyn. *Gangsters, Gunfire, and Political Intrigue: The Story of the Indiana State Police*. Indianapolis, IN: .38 Special Press, 2001.

Potter, Claire Bond. *War on Crime: Bandits, G-Men, and the Politics of Mass Culture*. New Brunswick. NJ: Rutgers University Press, 1998.

Poulson, Ellen. *Don't Call Us Molls: Women of the John Dillinger Gang*. Little Neck, NY: Clinton Cook Publishing, 2002.

Powers, Richard Gid. *Broken: The Troubled Past and Uncertain Future of the FBI*. New York: Free Press, 2004.

_____. *G-Men: Hoover's FBI in American Popular Culture*. Carbondale: Southern Illinois University Press, 1983.

_____. *Secrecy and Power: The Life of J. Edgar Hoover*. New York: Free Press of Glencoe, 1987.

Purvis, Alston, and Alex Tresniowski. *The Vendetta: FBI Hero Melvin Purvis's War against Crime, and J. Edgar Hoover's War against Him*. New York: Public Affairs, 2005.

Ruth, David E. *Inventing the Public Enemy: The Gangster in American Culture, 1918–1934*. Chicago: University of Chicago Press, 1996.

Schneider, Paul. *Bonnie and Clyde: The Lives behind the Legend*. New York: Henry Holt and Company, 2009.

Sissom, Carol. *Banking with Dillinger*. Indianapolis, IN: Carol's Adventures, 2009.

Stewart, Tony. *Dillinger the Hidden Truth: A Tribute to Gangsters and G-Men of the Great Depression Era*. Bloomington, IN: Tony Stewart Publication, 2010.

Theoharis, Athen G., and John Stuart Cox. *The Boss: J. Edgar Hoover and the Great American Inquisition*. Philadelphia: Temple University Press, 1988.

Toland, John. *The Dillinger Days*. New York: Da Capo Press, 1995.

Weiner, Tim. *Enemies: A History of the FBI*. New York: Random House, 2012.

Media/DVD

Manhattan Melodrama (1934). Metro-Goldwyn-Mayer.

Dillinger (1945). King Brothers Production.

The Woman in Red (1979). New World Pictures.

Dillinger and Capone (1995). Concorde-New Horizons.

John Dillinger: Public Enemy Number One (1995). Biography/A&E Channel.

Public Enemy Number 1: The Legendary Outlaw John Dillinger (2002). PBS/American Experience.

Crime Wave: 19 Months of Mayhem (2008). History Channel.

Public Enemies (2009). Universal Pictures.

Websites

FBI. http://www.fbi.gov/about-us/history/famous-cases/john-dillinger.

Biography Channel. http://www.thebiographychannel.co.uk/biographies/john-dillinger.html.

Public Broadcasting System. http://www.pbs.org/wgbh/amex/dillinger/.

John Dillinger-related Comic Books. http://www.comicvine.com/john-dillinger/4005-32248.

John Dillinger Scrapbook. http://jhdillinger.fortunecity.com/.

John Dillinger Museum. http://www.dillingermuseum.com/.

John Dillinger Biography. http://www.biography.com/people/john-dillinger-9274804.

Index